great songs... of the nineties

The

Any

Most musical decades wind up identified by at least one distinct sound signature. Often two sounds will dominate, one taking over mid-decade or so from the entrenched monotony of the earlier, once-vibrant other. The new sound not only wipes out the prevailing old sound, it also brings with it a vast assemblage of previously undiscovered talents, geniuses and copycats, innovators and journeymen alike, who through mutual self-interest, competitive desire, or pure coincidence have seemingly all been working independently toward the same object, until one larger-than-life breakthrough occurs, setting everyone else into motion.

Elvis did it in the 1950s, with rock 'n' roll abolishing pop to the ranks of nostalgia almost overnight. In the 1960s, the combination of the Beatles and Bob Dylan wrought folk/rock upon the college-age generation, relegating good old rock 'n' roll to the dustbins of antiquity. The 1970s, after a brief, quiet start, was dominated by rhythm and noise, disco and arena rock, knocking subtlety and reflection out the window. At the top of the 1980s, having temporarily danced ourselves into oblivion, we settled in to watch TV. The sound of MTV was the sound of a synthesized English invasion set to quirky yet memorable melodies.

The 1990s as a musical entity provided us with no such useful symmetry. As if preparing for the end of the millennium, the decade instead drew back in reflection, showcasing virtually every genre of music that had become popular in the forty years preceding it (and in some cases years before that), each one taking its turn in the heat of the spotlight as if they were part of some massive traveling variety show of the type Allen Freed once popularized, where fifteen acts had fifteen minutes each.

The 1990s began like the 1960s, with a war (in the Gulf) and music to protest it (Julie Gold's poignant "From a Distance," popularized by Bette Midler). In 1992, the election of a sax-honking, Elvis-loving, Arkansas-born, baby boom Democrat as President, saw the rise of country music on the charts and in the honky-tonks of America, typified by the two step omnipresence of "Achy Breaky Heart" by Billy Ray Cyrus. Late in 1993 and throughout 1994, the jangly alternative of guitar-based rock made its way back to prominence for the first time in decades, featuring the breathy odes of the Cranberries ("Linger"), the enduring strength of the Pretenders ("I'll Stand by You"), and the stark imagery of Soundgarden ("Black Hole Sun"). In 1996 there was another British Invasion, led by the Beatles-influenced Oasis ("Wonderwall"), the Stones-influenced Bush ("Glycerine"), and the Twiggy-influenced the Spice Girls ("Say You'll Be There"). And now, as the decade slouches toward its conclusion, we are witnessing a rebirth of the harmonizing boy-group (Hanson, 98 Degrees, Backstreet Boys, 'N Sync) not seen since the heyday of Dion & the Belmonts. In the meantime, the return of Swing has come and gone, the death of Broadway has been once again averted, chiefly through the works of Andrew Lloyd Webber (*Sunset Boulevard*) and Frank Wildhorn (*Jekyll & Hyde*, *The Scarlet Pimpernel*, *The Civil War*), and the soaring ballad has proved to be as timeless as young love in any era.

In this regard, the decade stands tall, with every genre providing its share of outsized epics, from the metal arenas of Bon Jovi ("Blaze of Glory"), Mr. Big ("To Be with You"), and Aerosmith ("Amazing") to the more intimate stages of the aforementioned Wildhorn ("This Is the Moment" from *Jekyll & Hyde*) and Lloyd Webber ("As If We Never Said Goodbye" from *Sunset Boulevard*). In the 1990's female singers stood out as never before, especially in the realm of the big ballad, with none bigger than Celine Dion, whether offering the definitive remake of "The Power of Love," or the defining anthem of the decade, "My Heart Will Go On," from the movie *Titanic*. But there were other diva moments provided by the eloquent Sarah McLachlan ("Building a Mystery"), the bluesy Tracy Chapman ("Give Me One Reason"), the earthy Paula Cole ("Where Have All the Cowboys Gone?"), the soaring Vanessa Williams ("Save the Best for Last"), the philosophically inclined TLC ("Waterfalls"), the inspirational tandem of Whitney Houston and Mariah Carey ("When You Believe"), and the exceedingly wronged Alanis Morissette ("You Oughta Know").

From Eric Clapton's heart-wrenching tribute to his son, "Tears in Heaven," to Meat Loaf's ode to fidelity, "I'd Do Anything for Love (But I Won't Do That)," male divas, defying the stereotype or perhaps evidencing true growth in this regard, were just as capable of touching our emotions in the 1990s.

Hootie & the Blowfish redefined the bar-room weeper ("Let Her Cry"). Dave Matthews couched his hip sentiments in jazz/rock ("Crash into Me"). The harmonious brilliance of Boyz II Men ("End of the Road") carried their song to a record-breaking (for its time) number of weeks at the top of the charts.

Thus, if Rod Stewart emerged in the 1990s as rock's answer to Tony Bennett with his interpretation of Van Morrison's "Have I Told You Lately," and Sting laid claim to Bing Crosby with the lulling "Fields of Gold," and Joshua Kadison restated the Perry Como credo with the lovely "Beautiful in My Eyes," one might safely presume, as we neared the year 2000, that the pop song spectrum had pretty much come full circle since 1950.

What new forms of music or major artists will emerge in the next millennium to blow it all out of the water is anybody's guess.

—Bruce Pollock

CONTENTS

Achy Breaky Heart (Don't Tell My Heart)

Words and Music by Don Von Tress

what a fool I've been and laugh and joke a - bout me on the
fist can tell my lip. He nev - er real - ly liked me an - y -
A
phone. You can tell my arms go
way. Or tell your Aunt Lou - ise. Tell
back to the farm. You can tell my feet to hit the
an - y - thing you please. My - self al - read - y knows I'm not o -
E
floor. Or you can tell my lips to
kay. Or you can tell my eyes to

tell my fin - ger - tips they won't be reach - ing out for you no
watch out for my mind. It might be walk - ing out on me to -
A
more.
day. But
Don't tell my heart, my
ach - y break - y heart. I just don't think he'd un - der -
E
stand. And if you tell my heart, my ach - y break - y heart, he

A
To Coda
might blow_ up and kill this man. Ooh.
E
1 A
2 A
D.S. al Coda
CODA
A
man.

Don't tell my heart, my ach - y break - y heart. _ I just don't think he'd un - der -
E
stand. And if you tell my heart, my ach - y break - y heart, _ he
A
might blow _ up and kill this man. Ooh. ___
E

A
E
A

Amazing (It's Amazing)

Words and Music by Steven Tyler and Richie Supa

F#m7b5
4 fr
F
1
2,3
try'n to walk through the pain. When I
wish-ing that I would die.
scratch-ing to stay a-live.
It's a-
C
Em7
F
C/E
maz-ing, with the blink of an eye you fin-'ly see the light.
G
C/G
G7
C
Em7
Oh, it's a-maz-ing, when the
F
C/E
G
C/G
mo-ment ar-rives that you know you'll be al-right.

G7
F
C/E
Yeah, Oh, it's a - maz - ing, and I'm
D7
G7sus
To Coda
C
say - ing a prayer_ for the des - per - ate hearts_ to - night._
G/B
Am
That one last shot's a per - ma - nent_ va - ca -
D7
F
- tion, And_ how high can you fly_ with bro - ken wings?_

C
G/B
Am
Life's a jour - ney, not a des - ti - na -
D7
F
G
C/G
G7
- tion, and I just can't tell just what to-mor-row brings.
D.S. al Coda
You have to
CODA
C
Dm
The
C/E
F
des-per-ate hearts, des-per-ate hearts. Vocal ad lib.

C
Guitar solo - ad lib.
Dm
C/E
F
C/G
Am
C/G
1-3
F
4
F
C
C7

Black Hole Sun

Words and Music by Chris Cornell

F5
Em
E♭
3fr
Dsus
black, the sky _ looks dead. _ Call me name _ through _ the cream, and _ I'll
youth I pray _ to keep. _ Heav-en send _ hell ___ a - way. No _ one
G6
Fdim
A♭
4fr
E♭sus
Dsus
hear you scream _ a - gain. _
sings like you _ an - y - more. _
Black hole sun, won't you come _ and
G
G5/F
B♭
E♭
3fr
D7
wash a - way _ the rain? _ Black hole sun, won't you come? _ Won't you come? _
1
C
D
_ Won't you come? _ Stut - ter - ___
2
C
B♭
Black hole

Eb
D7sus
G
G5/F
Bb
sun, won't you come and wash a - way the rain? Black hole
Eb
D7
C
Bb
sun, won't you come? Won't you come?
D
C
Bb
To Coda
Won't you come?
D
C
Bb
Won't you come?

D
C
B♭
Won't you come?
D
N.C.
Play 6 times
G/F
F5
G5
3 fr
Hang my
R.H.
G6
B♭6
F5
Em
D.S. al Coda
(take 2nd ending)
head, drown my fear, 'til you all just dis-ap - pear.
Black hole
CODA
D
C
B♭
Won't you come?

D
C
B♭
Won't you come?
D
C
B♭
Won't you come?
D
C
B♭
Won't you come?
D
N.C.
G/F
F5
G5
3 fr
R.H.

From SUNSET BOULEVARD

As If We Never Said Goodbye

Music by Andrew Lloyd Webber

Lyrics by Don Black and Christopher Hampton, with contributions by Amy Powers

Fm/E♭
E♭
E♭maj7
D♭maj7
ov-er-crowd-ed hall-ways, the at-mos-phere as thrill-ing here as al - ways.
L.H.
A♭/C
Fm7
Feel the ear-ly morn-ing mad - ness, feel the ma-gic in the mak - ing. Why,
E♭maj7/B♭
A♭/B♭
E♭
ev-ery-thing's as if we ne - ver said good - bye. I've
mf
E♭maj7
Fm/E♭
E♭
spent so ma-ny morn-ings, just try-ing to re-sist you. I'm trem-bling now, you

E♭maj7
D♭maj7
A♭/C
can't know how I've missed you, missed the fai-ry tale ad-ven-tures in this
Fm7
D♭
A♭/C
B♭7
ev-er-spin-ning play-ground. We were young to-geth-er, I'm
E♭maj7
A♭/E♭
E♭
com-ing out of make-up, the light's al-rea-dy burn-ing, not long un-til the
f
E♭maj7
D♭maj7
A♭/C
cam-eras will start turn-ing, and the ear-ly morn-ing mad-ness,

Fm
E♭maj7/B♭
and the ma-gic in the mak - ing,
yes, ev-ery-thing's as if we
Fm7/B♭
E♭
Gm7
Cm7
Gm7
ne - ver said good - bye.
I don't want to be a - lone, that's all in the
Cm7
B♭
Cm
Gm
Cm
past.
This world's wait - ed long e - nough, I've come home at
B♭7
E♭maj7
A♭/E♭
last, and this time will be big - ger, and bright-ter than we knew it.
f assai

E♭
E♭maj7
D♭maj7
So watch me fly, we all know I can do it. Could I
A♭/C
Fm7
stop my hand from shak - ing? Has there ev - er been a mo - ment with so
D♭
A♭/C
B♭7
E♭maj7
p
much to live for? The whis-pered con - ver - sa - tions in
Fm/E♭
E♭
E♭maj7
ov - er-crowd-ed hall - ways, so much to say, not just to - day, but

D♭maj7
A♭/C
al - ways. We'll have ear-ly morn-ing mad - ness, we'll have
L.H.
Fm
E♭maj7/B♭
A♭6/B♭
ma-gic in the mak - ing, yes, ev-ery-thing's as if we ne - ver said good -
Cm
Cm/A
E♭maj7/B♭
A♭6/B♭
B♭7
E♭
D♭/E♭
- bye, yes, ev-ery-thing's as if we ne - ver said good - bye.
A♭
B♭
E♭
B♭7
A♭/E♭
E♭
We taught the world new ways to dream.

Beautiful In My Eyes

Words and Music by Joshua Kadison

E♭/B♭
6fr
B♭
You're my
We'll have our
we can
A♭maj7
B♭/A♭
Mo - na Li - sa, you're my rain - bow skies, and my
fill of tears, our share of sighs. My
laugh a - bout how time real - ly flies. We won't
Gm7
3fr
Cm7
3fr
on - ly prayer is that you re - al - ize
on - ly prayer is that you re - al - ize
say good - bye 'cause true love nev - er dies;
Fm7
E♭/G
3fr
A♭(add9)
3fr
B♭sus
B♭
you'll al - ways be beau - ti - ful in my

1
2,3
Eb
Eb/Bb
Bb
3 fr
6 fr
eyes.
eyes. You will al - ways
be beau-ti-ful in my eyes.
Ab/Eb
And the pass - ing years will show that you will al - ways
Ab
Eb/G
4 fr
Fm7
To Coda
grow ev - er more beau - ti - ful in my

E♭ Fm7 E♭/G A♭sus2 B♭
D.S. al Coda
(Take 2nd ending)
eyes.
When there are
CODA
E♭ B♭
eyes. The pass - ing years_ will show_ that you will al - ways
A♭ E♭/G Fm7 B♭ E♭ Fm7
grow_ ev - er more_ beau - ti - ful_ in my eyes.
E♭/G A♭sus2 B♭ E♭
rit.

Believe

Words by Lenny Kravitz
Music by Lenny Kravitz and Henry Hirsch

E+
Bm/D
Am/C
G
D
If you want it, you got to be - lieve.
If you want it you got to be - lieve.
mf
A
F
Who are we? We're who we are,
'Cause be - ing free is a state of mind.
The fu - ture's in our pres- ent hands.
mp
A
F
rid - ing on this great big star.
We'll one day leave this all be - hind.
Let's reach right in, let's un - der- stand.

E+
Bm/D
Am/C
G
D
We've got to stand up if we're gon - na be free, yeah.
Just put your faith in God, and one day you'll see, yeah.
If you want it, you got to be - lieve, yeah.
mf
B♭
F/A
Gm7
3fr.
F
If you want it you got it, you just got to be - lieve,
f
C/E
Cm/E♭
C
F
be - lieve in your - self.
B♭
F/A
Gm7
3fr.
F
'Cause it's all just a game, we just want to be loved.

To Coda
C/E
Cm/E♭
E
1.
mf
2.
D.S. al Coda
Coda
Am
F
G
Em7
F
Dm7
G
3
Repeat and fade

Black Velvet

Words and Music by Christopher Ward and David Tyson

Jim- mie Rod - gers on the Vic - trola up high.
"White Light - nin'" bound to drive you wild.
Ma - ma's danc - in' with ba - by on her shoul - der.
Ma - ma's ba - by is in the heart of ev - 'ry school girl.
The sun is set - tin' like mo - las - ses in the sky.
"Love Me Ten - der" leaves 'em cry - in' in the aisle.
B7sus
B7
A7sus
A7
The boy could sing; knew how to move ev - 'ry - thing.
The way he moved it was a sin so sweet and true.

G7sus
G7
Dsus
Al- ways want- ing more.
He'd leave you long - ing for
Am9
D
Black vel - vet and that lit - tle boy smile.
Am9
F
C
Black vel - vet {with / and} that slow south-ern style.
Am9
D
A new re - li - gion that - 'll bring you to your knees.

1
C7
B7sus 4
Em
Black vel - vet, if you please.
2
C7
B7sus 4
Black vel - vet, if you
Em
please.
Am
Ev-'ry word of ev-'ry song
B7
Em7
that he sang was for you.

Am
F
In a flash he was gone it hap - pened so
C
B7
soon.
What could you do?
Em7

Am7
Am9
Black vel - vet and that
D
Am7
Am9
lit - tle boy smile.
Black vel - vet in that
F
C
Am7
Am9
slow south-ern style.
A new re - li - gion that - 'll
D
1
C7
B7sus4
bring you to your knees.
Black vel - vet,

Em
2
C7
B7sus
if you please.
Black vel - vet, if you
Em7
please.
If you please.
If you please.
If you please.
Mm.
Mm.
1
2
Repeat ad lib. and Fade

Building A Mystery

Words and Music by Sarah McLachlan and Pierre Marchand

D
A
Bm
G
su - i - cide po - em and a cross from a faith that died
D
A
E5
G
Asus/E A/E
be - fore Je - sus came. You're build - ing a mys - ter - y.
Bm
G
D
Asus
A
You
Bm
G
D
A
live in a church where you sleep with voo - doo dolls, and you
scream-ing a - loud a prayer from your se - cret god to

Bm
G
D
A
won't give up the search for the ghost in the halls.
feed off of fears and hold back your tears, oh.
Bm
G
D
A
You wear san - dals in the snow and a smile I won't wash - a - way.
You give us a tan - trum and a know - it - all grin,
Bm
G
D
A
3
Can you look out the win - dow with - out your shad - ow get - ting in the way?
just when you need one when the eve - ning stayed.
Esus
E
G(add9)
You're so beau - ti - ful, with an edge and charm - ing.
You're a beau - ti - ful, a beau - ti - ful fucked - up man.

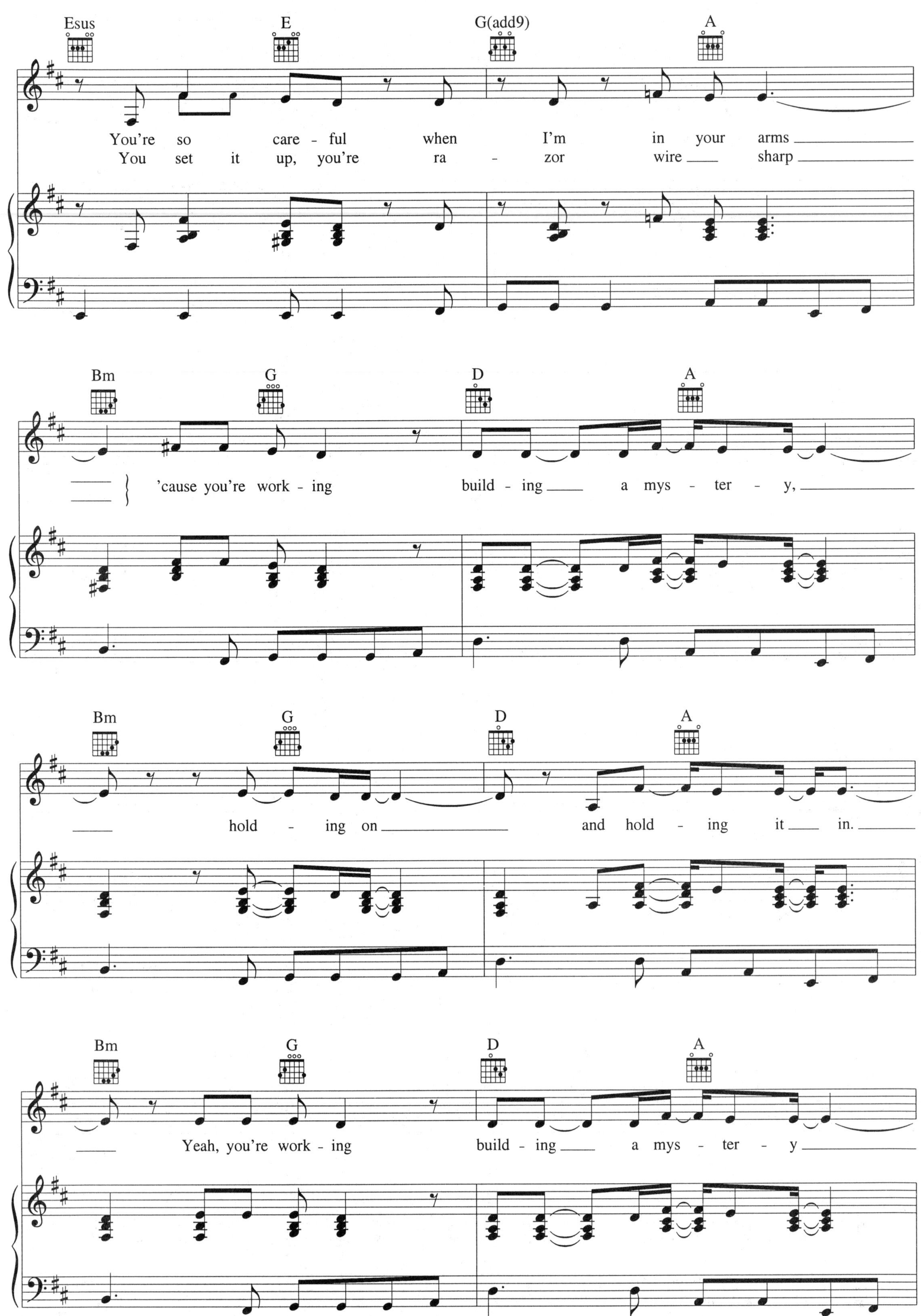
Esus
E
G(add9)
A
You're so care - ful when I'm in your arms
You set it up, you're ra - zor wire sharp
Bm
G
D
A
'cause you're work - ing build - ing a mys - ter - y,
Bm
G
D
A
hold - ing on and hold - ing it in.
Bm
G
D
A
Yeah, you're work - ing build - ing a mys - ter - y

Bm
G
1 D
A
and choos - ing so care - ful - ly.
Asus
A
2 D
A
You woke up
care - ful - ly.
G
A
Gmaj9
4 fr
E5
Guitar solo
G
Asus
G
A
G
Gmaj9
4 fr
Solo ends

E5
G
A
Ooh, you're work - ing build - ing a mys - ter - y,
Bm
G
D
A
hold - ing on and hold - ing it in.
Bm
G
D
A
Yeah, you're work - ing build - ing a mys - ter - y
Bm
G
D
A
Bm
G
and choos - ing so care - ful - ly. Yeah, you're work-ing

D
A
Bm
G
build - ing a mys - ter - y,
hold - ing on
D
A
Bm
G
and hold - ing it in.
Oh yeah, you're work - ing
D
A
Bm
G
D
A
build - ing a mys - ter - y
and choos - ing so
care - ful - ly.
Bm7
2 fr
G
D
Asus
You're build - ing a mys - ter - y.
rit.

Featured in the film YOUNG GUNS II

Blaze Of Glory

Words and Music by Jon Bon Jovi

G
Dm
old coat for a pil-low and the earth was last night's bed. I
look-ing for for-give-ness but be-fore I'm six feet deep, Lord,
F
C
To Coda
don't know where I'm go-ing, on-ly God knows where I've been. I'm a
I got to ask a fa-vor and I hope you'll un-der-stand. 'Cause I've
G
Dm
dev-il on the run, a six-gun lov-er, a can-dle in the wind, yeah!
D5
mf

Dm
When you're brought in - to this world _ they
ask a - bout _ my con-science and I
C
G
say you're born in sin. Well, at least they gave me some - thing I did-n't have to
of - fer you my soul. You ask if I'll grow to be _ a wise ___ man, well I
Dm
F
steal or have _ to win. Well, they tell me that _ I'm want - ed, yeah,
ask if I'll _ grow old. You ask me if ___ I've known love and what it's like to
C
G
I'm a want - ed man. ___ I'm a colt in your sta-ble, I'm what Cain was to A-bel. Mis-ter
sing songs in the rain. _ Well, I've seen love come, I've seen it shot down, I've

Dm
G
catch me if you can. I'm go-ing
seen it die in vain. Shot
down in a blaze of glo-
D
G
-ry. Take me now but know the truth.
D
G
I'm go-ing out
'Cause I'm go-ing down
I'm go-ing out
in a blaze of
D
C
To Coda II
glo-ry. Lord, I nev-er drew first but I drew first blood,
and I'm
I'm the
and I'm

G
1
D5
no-one's son. Call me young _ gun.
de-vil's son. Call me young _
2
D5
You
gun.
G
D
F
Play 3 times
Guitar solo ad lib.

G
no chord
D5
Solo ends
D.S. al Coda
Each
CODA
G
Dm
lived life to the full-est let this boy_ die like a man.
G
Dm
Star-ing down a bul-let, let me make_ my fin-al stand.
rit.

D.S.S. al Coda II
Shot
a tempo
f
CODA II
G
no - one's son, call me young
D
C
gun.
3
I'm a young gun.
G
D
Young
C
gun,
yeah, yeah, yeah, young

Additional Lyrics (Album version)

2. When you're brought into this world
   They say you're born in sin.
   Well, at least they gave me something
   I didn't have to steal or have to win.
   Well, they tell me that I'm wanted
   Yeah, I'm a wanted man.
   I'm a colt in your stable,
   I'm what Cain was to Abel.
   Mister, catch me if you can.

From THE CIVIL WAR

Candle In The Window

Words by Jack Murphy
Music by Frank Wildhorn

G6/9
burn - ing in a win - dow near a fig - ure in a chair,
Ti - red of the de - mons, he must sit up there and fight,
he will keep his can - dle burn - ing just a mo - ment more,
al - ways sit - ting there,
deep in - to the night,
till he finds a way.
1.
D6/9
qui - et as a prayer.
2.
Omit 2nd time
D6/9
pray - ing that he's right.
This is what I pray.
Ev - 'ry
And I

Cadd2
G/B
A/D
D
A/D
D
eve - ning I can see his shad - ow on the shade, and I
won - der, does he see me pass - ing by each night, as
Cadd2
G/B
Asus4
don't feel so a - lone or so a - fraid.
I look up to find his patch of light?
A
Dmaj7
Am
B7
There's a can - dle in the win - dow ev - 'ry
Em7
Gm
A7
Dsus4
D
night, re - flect - ing all our hopes and dreams, or

Bm7
G
A
so it seems to me, as I look up to see that
Dmaj7
Am
B7
Em7
Gm
A7
can - dle in the win - dow ev 'ry night.
shin - ing bright.
Burn - ing like the yearn-
A little slower
Dsus4
D
Bm9
ing to be free,
far a - way and dim,
Tempo I
D/C
D6/9
kept a - live by him.

To Coda
D.S. (take 2nd ending) al Coda
Coda
D6/9
Hur - ry through the night
towards a
sol - i - tar - y light.
D6/9
Repeat and fade

Crash Into Me

Words and Music by David J. Matthews

E5/G♯ Asus2 E5/B E5 C♯m7 Asus2
to me tight. Tie me up a - gain. Who's got the claws in
E5/B E5 E5/G♯ Asus2 E5/B E5
you, my friend? In - to your heart I'll beat a - gain.
C♯m7 Asus2 E5/B E5 E5/G♯ Asus2
Sweet like can - dy to my soul. Sweet you rock and
E5/B E5 C♯m7 Asus2 E5/B E5
sweet you roll. Lost for you, I'm so lost

E5/G♯
Asus2
E5/B
E5
for you.
Oh, and you come
Chorus
C♯m7
N.C.
E
D/F♯
crash
in - to me.
And I come in - to
C♯m7
Asus2
E5/B
E5
E5/G♯
Asus2
you,
E5/B
E5
C♯m7
Asus2
E5/B
E5
and I come in - to you.

E5/G♯
Asus2
E5/B
E5
In a boy's dream,
C♯m7
in a boy's
dream.
Asus2
E5/B
E5
E5/G♯
Asus2
E5/B
E5

C♯m7
Asus2
E5/B
E5
2. Touch your lips just so I know.
3. See additional lyrics
E5/G♯
Asus2
E5/B
E5
In your eyes, love, it glows so. I'm
C♯m7
Asus2
E5/B
E5
bare - boned and cra - zy for
E5/G♯
Asus2
E5/B
E5
you.
Oh, when you come

Chorus
C♯m7
N.C.
E
crash in - to me, yeah, ba -
D/F♯
C♯m7
Asus2
by. And I come in - to
E5/B
E5
E5/G♯
Asus2
you.
1.
E5/B
E5
C♯m7
In a boy's dream,

Asus2
E5/B
in a boy's dream.
E5
E5/G♯
Asus2
E5/B
E5
2.
E5/B
E5
Oh,
C♯m7
Asus2
E5/B
E5
hike up your skirt a lit - tle more
and show the

E5/G♯
Asus2
E5/B
E5
world to me.
C♯m7
Asus2
E5/B
E5
3
Hike up your skirt a lit - tle more and show your
E5/G♯
Asus2
E5/B
E5
world to me.
In a boy's dream,
C♯m7
Asus2
E5/B
E5
in a boy's dream.

E5/G♯
Asus2
E5/B
E5
Oh,
C♯m7
Asus2
E5/B
E5
I watch you there, through the win - dow, and I stare at you
E5/G♯
Asus2
E5/B
E5
wear nothing, but you wear it so well.
C♯m7
Asus2
E5/B
E5
Tied up and twist - ed, the way I like to be. For

E5/G♯
Asus2
E5/B
E5
you,
for me,
come
crash
in - to me,
ba -
C♯m7
Asus2
E5/B
E5
by.
Come
crash
in - to me,
yeah,
E5/G♯
Asus2
E5/B
E5
yeah.
Crash

Additional Lyrics

3. Only if I've gone overboard,
   Then I'm begging you
   To forgive me, oh,
   In my haste.
   When I'm holding you so, girl,
   Close to me.
   Oh, and you come... *(To Chorus)*

Champagne Supernova

Words and Music by Noel Gallagher

A/E
A
A/G
slow-ly walk-ing down the hall
fast-er than a can-non ball,
A/F♯
A/E
where were you while we were get-ting high.
Some day you will
A
A/G
find me caught be-neath the land - slide,
in a cham-
A/F♯
A/E
A
- pagne su-per-no - va in the sky.
Some day you will find me caught be-neath the land-

A/G
A/F♯
- slide,
in a cham - pagne su - per - no - va, a
A/E
A
A/G
cham - pagne su - per - no - va in the sky.
A/F♯
A/E
A
1. Wake up the dawn and ask her why, a
(Verse 2 see block lyric)
A/G
A/F♯
dream - er dreams she ne - ver dies,
wipe that tear a - way now from your eyes.

A/E
A
A/G
Slow-ly walk-ing down the hall, fast-er than a can-non ball,
A/F♯
E
where were you while we were get-ting high.
Some day you will
A
A/G
find me caught be-neath the land - slide,
in a cham-
A/F♯
A/E
A
-pagne su-per-no - va in the sky.
Some day you will find me caught be-neath the land-

A/G
A/F♯
E
- slide, in a cham - pagne su-per-no - va, a cham-pagne su-per-no - va. 'Cause
D
peo - ple be - lieve that they're gon - na get a - way for the sum -
A
G
- mer but you and I we live and die the
D
E
E7
world's still spin - ning round, we don't know why, why, why, why, why.

1.
A
A/G
A/F♯
A/E
2.
Fmaj7
G
play 4 times

Fmaj7
G
Fmaj7
G
A
A/G
A/F♯
A/E
A
A/G
A/F♯
A/E
A
A/G
How ma - ny spe - cial peo - ple change—
how ma - ny lives are liv - ing strange,—

Verse 2:
How many special people change
How many lives are living strange
Where were you while we were getting high?
Slowly walking down the hall
Faster than a cannon ball
Where were you while we were getting high?

Featured on the Motion Picture Soundtrack PHENOMENON

Change The World

Words and Music by Gordon Kennedy, Wayne Kirkpatrick and Tommy Sims

A/E
E7(no3rd)
shine it on my heart
I'd take you as my queen,
A/E
E
so you could see the truth.
I'd have it no oth - er way.
A
D/A
A7(no3rd)
2fr
Then this love I have in - side
And our love will rule in this
D/A
A
is ev - 'ry - thing it seems,
king - dom we have made.

E
A/E
E7(no3rd)
but for now I find
'Til then I'd be a fool
A/E
G#7
4 fr
's on - ly in my dreams
wish - ing for the day
that I can
F#m7
G#7
C#m7
change the world.
D#m7♭5
G#7
C#m
I will would would be the sun - light in your u - ni - verse.

D♯m7♭5
G♯7
C♯m
Cm
Bm9
You would think my love was real - ly some - thing good, ba - by,
A
E(add9)/G♯
To Coda
1
Edim/G
F♯m7
if I could change the world.
E
A/E
Em7
A/E
E
2
Edim/G
F♯m7
change the world,

E
A7sus
E(add9)/G#
Edim/G F#m7(add4)
2fr
ba - by, if I could change
A/E
G
the world. Guitar solo
F#m7
4fr
G#7
D.S. al Coda
Solo ends I could

CODA
Edim/G
F♯m7
A
E(add9)/G♯
change the world, ba - by, if I could
Edim/G
F♯m7
A
E(add9)/G♯
E(add9)/G♯
Edim/G
change the world, ba - by, if I could change
Esus/F♯
G6
E
F♯m7
G
the world.
F♯m7
E

From the Paramount Motion Picture BOOMERANG

End Of The Road

Words and Music by Babyface, L.A. Reid and Daryl Simmons

Ab
Gm7
Fm7
Bb9sus
4 fr
3 fr
4 fr
Why do you play with my heart? Why do you play with my mind?
You've nev - er been there be - fore, it's on - ly your first time.
Eb
Ebsus
Eb
Bb/C
Cm
3 fr
You said we'd be for - ev - er, said it'd nev - er die.
May - be I'll for - give you, may - be you'll try.
Ab
Gm7
Fm7
Bb9sus
How could you love me and leave me and nev - er say good - bye? Well, I
We should be hap - py to - geth - er, for - ev - er, you and I. Could you
Cm
Cm/B
Eb/Bb
Am7b5
6 fr
can't sleep at night with - out hold - ing you tight. Girl, each time I try I just break down and cry.
love me a - gain like you loved me be - fore? This time I want you to love me much more.

A♭maj7
Gm7
Fm7
A♭maj7/B♭
(1.) Pain in my head, oh, I'd rath-er be dead, spin-nin' a-round and a-round.
(2.,3.) This time in-stead, just come to my bed and, ba-by, just don't let me down.
Al-though we've
E♭
E♭sus
B♭/C
Cm
come to the end of the road, still I can't let you
A♭
go. It's un-nat-u-ral. You be-long to me, I be-long to you.
Come to the end of the road, still I can't let you
3fr
4fr

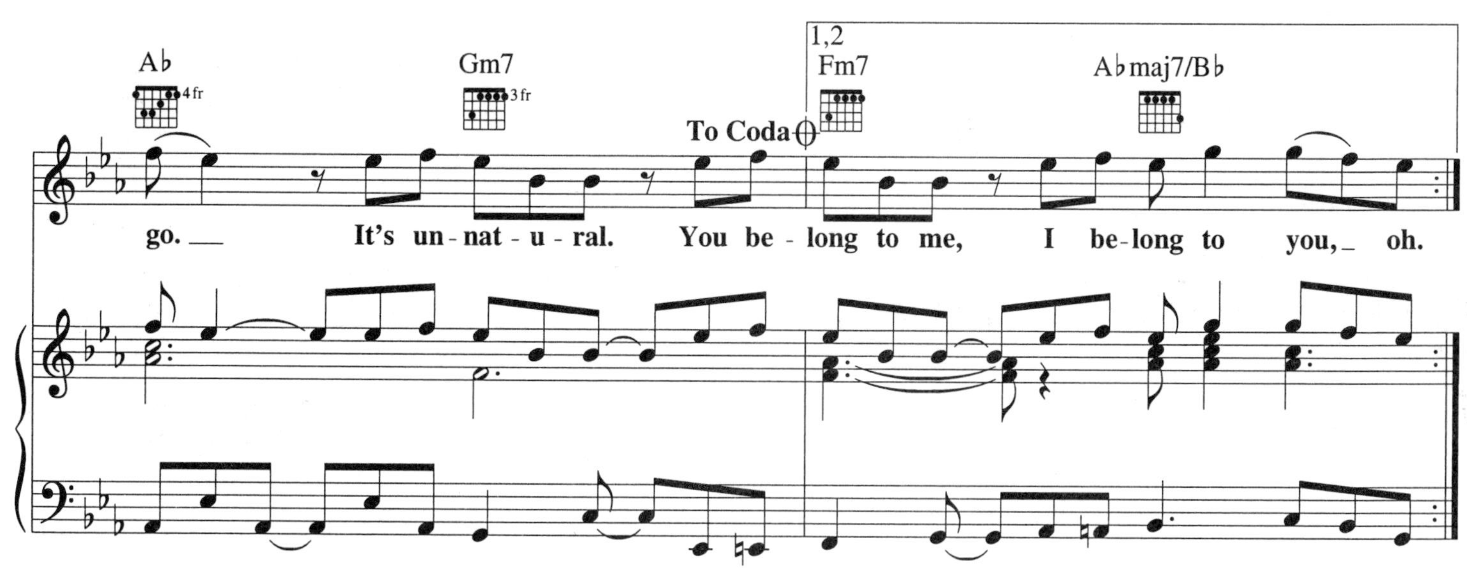

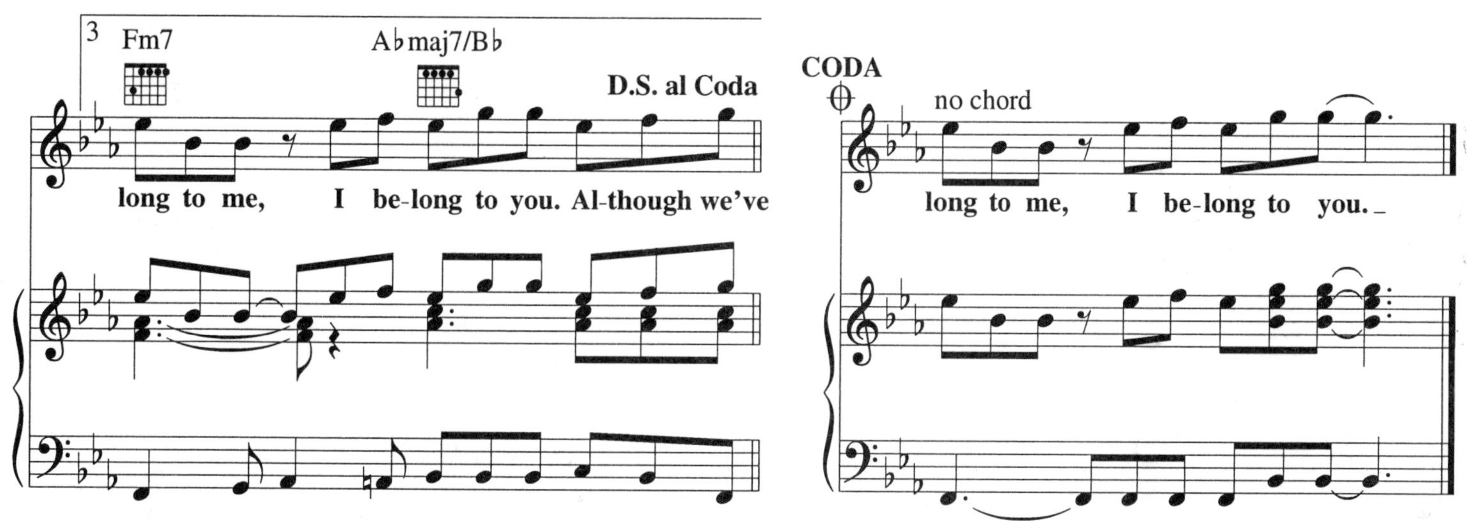

Additional lyrics

(Spoken:) Girl, I'm here for you.
All those times at night when you just hurt me,
And just ran out with that other fellow,
Baby, I knew about it.
I just didn't care.
You just don't understand how much I love you, do you?
I'm here for you.
I'm not out to go out there and cheat all night just like you did, baby.
But that's alright, huh, I love you anyway.
And I'm still gonna be here for you 'til my dyin' day, baby.
Right now, I'm just in so much pain, baby.
'Cause you just won't come back to me, will you?
Just come back to me.

Yes, baby, my heart is lonely.
My heart hurts, baby, yes, I feel pain too.
Baby please...

Fields Of Gold

Written and Composed by Sting

G
D
G/B
A
Bm7
2 fr
jeal - ous sky as we walk in fields of gold.
jeal - ous sky as we lie in fields of gold.
3
G
D
So she
See the
Bsus
2 fr
G
took her love for to gaze a - while up - on the fields of bar -
west wind move like a lov - er so up - on the fields of bar -
D
Bsus2
7 fr
G
D
- ley. In his arms she fell as her hair came down a - mong
- ley. Feel her bod - y rise when you kiss her mouth a - mong

G/B
A
1
D
2
D
the fields of gold.
Will you
the fields of gold.
G
D
G
I nev - er made prom - is - es light - ly,
and there have been
D
G
D
some that I've bro - ken,
but I swear in the days still left we'll walk
G/B
A
D
G/B
A
in fields of gold.
We'll walk in fields of gold.

D
Bsus2
7 fr
G
D
Bsus2
7 fr
G
D
3
G/B
A
D
Bsus2
7 fr
Man - y years have passed since those
mem - ber me when the
G
D
sum - mer days a - mong the fields of bar - ley. See the
west wind moves up - on the fields of bar - ley. You can

Bsus2
7 fr
G
D
G/B
A
chil - dren run as the sun goes down a - mong the fields of gold.
tell the sun in his jeal - ous sky when we walked in fields of gold,
1
D
2
D
G/B
A
You'll re -
when we walked in fields of gold,
D
G/B
A
D
G/D
D
when we walked in fields of gold.
G/D
D
G/D
D
1
G/D
D
2

From A Distance

Words and Music by Julie Gold

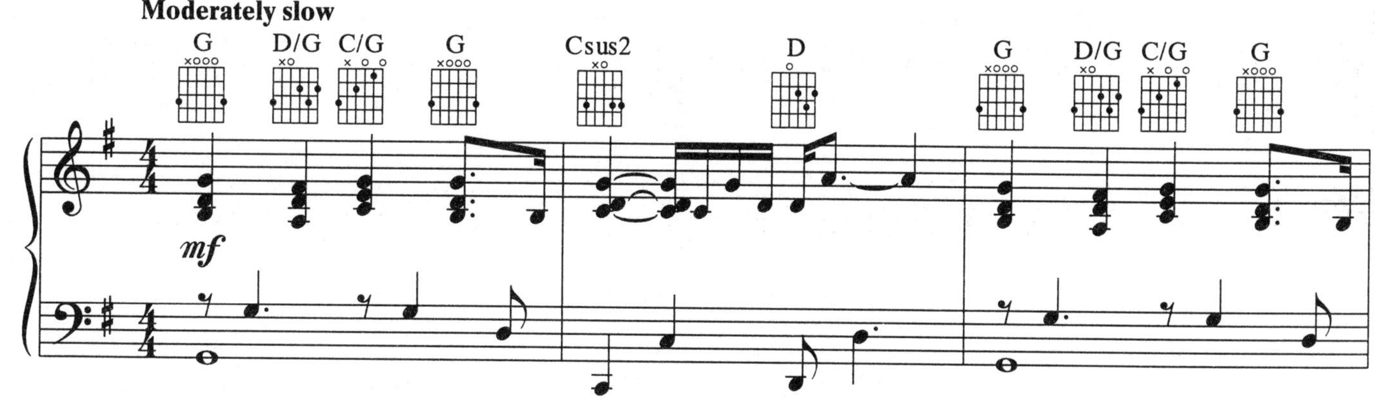

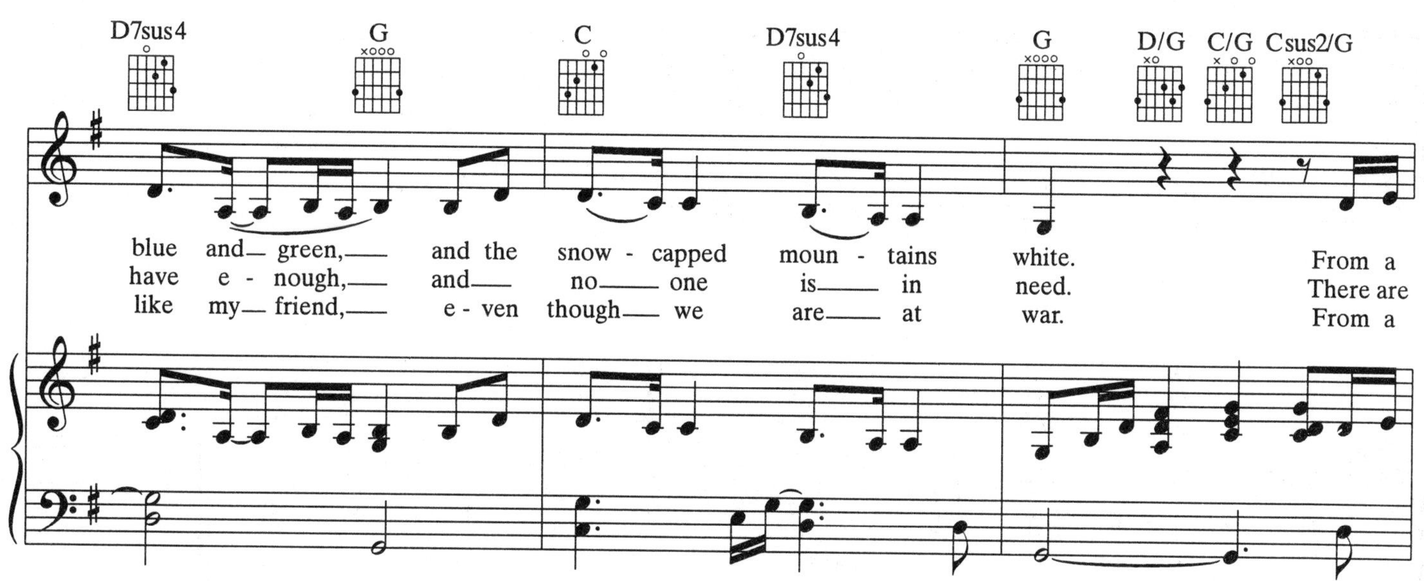

Play 1st time only
G
C
D7sus4
G
dis - tance the o - cean meets the stream, and the
Play 2nd and 3rd times only
G
C
D7sus4
Em
no guns, no bombs, no dis - eas - es, no
dis - tance I can't com - pre - hend what
C
D7sus4
G
D/G
G
ea - gle takes to flight. From a
hun - gry mouths to feed. From a
all this war is for. From a

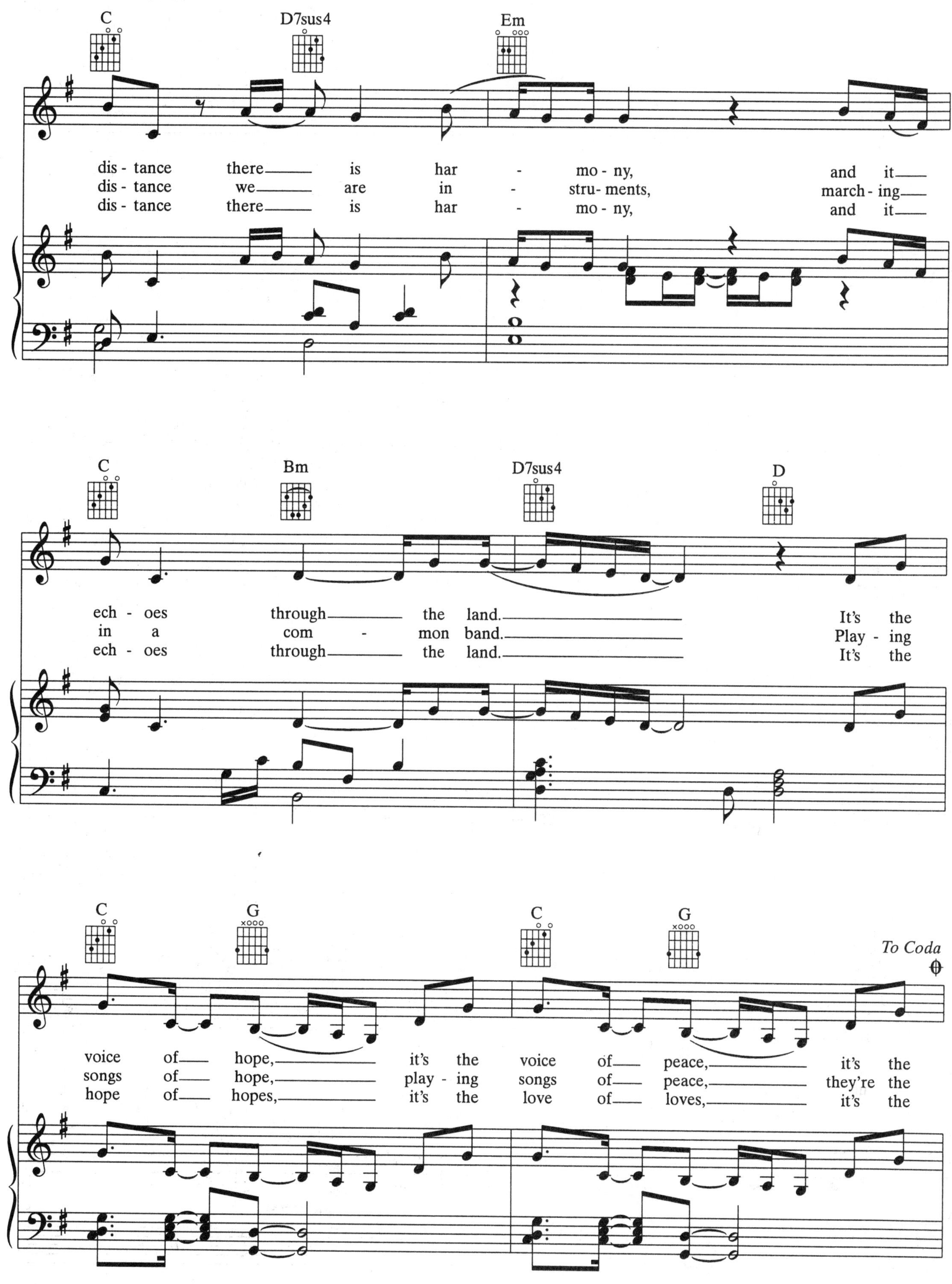
C
D7sus4
Em
dis - tance there is har - mo - ny, and it
dis - tance we are in - stru - ments, march - ing
dis - tance there is har - mo - ny, and it
C
Bm
D7sus4
D
ech - oes through the land. It's the
in a com - mon band. Play - ing
ech - oes through the land. It's the
C
G
C
G
To Coda
voice of hope, it's the voice of peace, it's the
songs of hope, play - ing songs of peace, they're the
hope of hopes, it's the love of loves, it's the

1.
C
D7sus4
G
D/G
C/G
G
Csus2
D
voice of ev - 'ry man.
songs of ev - 'ry
From a
2. G
D/G
G
C
D7sus4
G
Em
man.
God is watch-ing us, God is watch-ing us, God is
Am7
D7sus4
G
D/G
C/G
G
Csus2
D
watch-ing us from a dis-tance.
G
G/B
Csus2
D7sus4
G
G/B

Csus2
D
G
D/G
C/G
G
Csus2
D
D.S. al Coda
From a
Coda
C
D7sus4
Em
heart of ev - 'ry man.
It's the
C
G
C
G
hope of hopes, it's the love of loves, it's the
C
D7sus4
G
D/G
C/G
G
C
G/C
D7sus4
G
song of ev - 'ry man.

Give Me One Reason

Words and Music by Tracy Chapman

G
C
D
Give me one rea-son to stay here and I'll turn right back a -
G
C
round. __
Give me one rea-son to stay here __
D
G
and I'll turn right back a - round. _
Said I
D
C
G
don't want to leave you lone - ly; __
you _ got to make me change my _ mind. _

C
D
Ba-by, I got your num - ber.
want no one to squeeze me.
youth - ful heart can love you,
Ba-by, just give me one rea - son.
Oh, and I know that you got
They might take a - way my
Yes, and give you what you
Oh, give me just one rea - son
G
C
mine.
life.
need.
why.
But you know that I called you.
I don't want no one to squeeze me.
I said this youth - ful heart can love you,
Ba-by, just give me one rea - son.
D
G
I called too man - y times.
They might take a - way my life.
oh, and give you what you need.
Oh, give me just one rea - son why I should stay.

D
To Coda
You can call me, ba - by. You can
I just want some - one to hold me,
But I'm too old to go chas-ing you a -
Said I told you that I loved you,
1-3
C
G
call me an - y - time. But you got to call me.
oh, and rock me through the night.
round, wast-ing my pre - cious en - er - gy.
G
C
D
G
(1.,3.)Give me one rea-son to stay here and I'll turn right back a - round.
(2nd time - Instrumental solo)

C
D
(You could see me turn-ing.)
Give me one rea-son to stay here
and I'll turn right back a-
G
D
round.
(You could see me turn-ing.) Said I
don't want to leave you lone-ly;
C
G
Repeat 2 times, then D.S. al Coda
you got to make me change my mind.
(End solo)
I don't
This
CODA
C
N.C.
G7
and there ain't no more to say.
rit.

Glycerine

Words and Music by Gavin Rossdale

F
C
Dm
B♭
Don't let the days go by. Glyc-er-ine.
Glyc-er-ine.
I'm nev-er a-lone, but I'm a-lone all the time. Are you at
one, or do you lie? We live in a wheel where ev-'ry-one

Dm
B♭
F
steals. But when we rise, it's like Straw-ber-ry Fields. If I treat-ed you bad,
C
Dm
B♭
F
you bruise my face. Could-n't love you more. You've got a beau-ti-ful taste.
C
Dm
B♭
F
Don't let the days go by. Could have been
C
Dm
B♭
eas-i-er on you. I could-n't change, though I want-ed to.

F
C
Dm
B♭
Should have been eas - i - er by three, our old friend fear and you and me.
F
C
B♭
F
C
B♭
Glyc- er- ine.
Glyc- er- ine.
F
C
Dm
B♭
Don't let the days go by.
Glyc- er - ine.
F
C
Dm
B♭
Don't let the days go by.

F
C
Dm
B♭
Ah.
F
C
Dm
B♭
Glyc- er- ine.
Glyc- er- ine.
F
C
Dm
B♭
Oh,
glyc- er- ine.
Glyc- er- ine.
Dm
B♭
Dm
B♭
Bad moon wine a- gain.
Bad moon wine a- gain,
and she falls

F
C
a-round me.
I need-ed you more when you want-ed us
Dm
B♭
F
less. Could not kiss, just re - gress. It might just be
C
Dm
B♭
clear, sim-ple and plain. Well, that's just fine. That's just one of my names.
F
C
Dm
B♭
Don't let the days go by.

F
C
Dm
B♭
Could have been eas - i - er on you, you, you. Glyc- er- ine.
F
C
B♭
F
C
B♭
Glyc- er- ine.
Glyc- er- ine.
F
C
B♭
F
C
B♭
Glyc- er- ine.
F
Slowly
N.C.

From TITANIC – THE MUSICAL

Godspeed Titanic (Sail On)

Music and Lyrics by Maury Yeston

Gm
Dm
berth glide free!
E♭/F
F7add4
E♭
E♭/G
F7/A
As you plow the
B♭
B♭/D
D7sus4
D7
deep, in your arms I'll
Gm
Gm/F
B♭/C
C7
keep. Safe - ly west may you car -

C
E♭/F
F7add4
F/G
G7add4
ry me.
Sail
molto rit.
C
G/B
Am
Em
on, sail on, great ship
F
G7sus4
C
G/B
Ti - tan - ic. Cross the
Am
Em
o - pen sea!

F/G
G7add4
F
F/A
G7/B
Pray the jour - ney's
C
C/E
E7sus4
E7
sound till your port be
Am
Am/G
Fmaj9
Dm7
found. For - tune's winds sing God -
C/G
G7sus4
F♯m7♭5
speed to thee.

C/G
For - tune's winds sing God -
G7sus4
C
C/G
speed to thee!
rit.
fff a tempo
G
N.C.
D♭/C
D/C
E♭/C
E/C
C
Ped.

Have I Told You Lately

Words and Music by Van Morrison

Cm7
3fr
B♭
E♭/F
ease my trou-bles that's what you do.
For the
Instrumental
B♭
Dm7
E♭
3fr
E♭/F
morn - in' sun in all its glo - ry greets the
B♭
Dm7
E♭
3fr
E♭/F
day with hope and com-fort, too.
E♭maj7
3fr
Dm7
You fill my life with laugh - ter and some-how you make it bet - ter,

Cm7
Eb/F
Bb
Cm7
Bb/D
ease my trou-bles that's what you do.
Solo ends
Ebmaj7
There's a love that's di-vine
and it's yours and it's mine
Dm7
like the sun.
Cm7
Dm7
Ebmaj7
And at the end of the day
Dm7
we should give thanks and pray
to the one,
1
Eb/F
to the one.
Have I

2
Eb/F
Bb
Dm7
to the one. And have I told you late - ly that I
Eb
Eb/F
Bb
Dm7
love you? Have I told you there's no one else a -
Eb
Eb/F
Ebmaj7
bove you? You fill my heart with glad - ness,
Dm7
Cm7
Eb/F
take a - way my sad - ness, ease my trou-bles that's what you

B♭
Cm7
B♭/D
E♭maj7
3 fr
do.
Take a - way all ___ my sad - ness,
Dm7
Cm7
Cm7
B♭/D
fill my life _ with glad - ness,
ease my trou-bles that's _ what you do.
E♭maj7
Dm7
Take a - way all ___ my sad - ness,
fill my heart with glad - ness,
Cm7
E♭/F
ease my trou - bles that's ___ what you do.
rall.

Here And Now

Words and Music by Terry Steele and David Elliot

G(add9)/B
B7/D♯
Em7
G/B
Cmaj9
Hold-ing you close through the night,
I need you.
C/D
G(add9)
Yeah.
I look in your
I look in your
F♯m7♭5
B7♭9
Em7
D
eyes, and there I see what
eyes, there I see
C(add9)
C/D
G(add9)
hap - pi - ness real - ly means. The love that we
all that a love should real - ly be. And I need you

F♯m7♭5
4fr
B7♭9
Cmaj7
G/B
share makes life so sweet. To -
more and more each day.
C(add9)/E
Cm6/E♭
G/D
C(add9)
geth - er we'll al - ways be.
Noth - ing can take your love a - way.
G(add9)/B
B7/D♯
Em7
G/B
This pledge of love feels so right, and ooh, I need
More that I dare to dream. I need
Cmaj9
F♯m7♭5
4fr
A/B
you. Yeah.
you.
Here and now,

Cmaj9
D/C
D/F♯
G
G/B
I promise to love faithfully.
Cmaj9
F♯m7♭5
4 fr
A/B
Cmaj9
You're all I need.
Here and now, I
D/C
D/F♯
G
G/B
Cmaj9
To Coda
vow to be one with thee.
1
C/D
G
G/B
C
C/D
Your love is all I need.
Stay.

G(add9)
G/B
C
C/D
2 C
C/D
When Your love is all I
Cmaj9
D/C
D
need. Start-ing here, ooh, and I'm start - ing now. I be - lieve.
G
Cmaj9
Start - ing here, I'm start - ing right here. Start - ing now,
(I be - lieve.)
C/D
right now, be-cause I be - lieve in your love, so I'm

F/G
G/B
Cmaj9
D.S. al Coda
glad to take the vow. Here and now, oh, I
CODA
C/D
G(add9)
Your love is all I, need.
I, yeah,
Vocal ad lib.
G(add9)/B
Cmaj9
1,2
B♭maj9
Cmaj9
Fmaj9
yeah. Uh, yeah. Ay ah, love is all I
last time rit.
3
B♭maj9
C(add9)
G(add9)
Yeah.

Hold My Hand

Words and Music by Darius Carlos Rucker, Everett Dean Felber,
Mark William Bryan and James George Sonefeld

Bsus2
E
Bsus2
E
peace ___ and some har - mo - ny ___
"Get _ up and let me see you smile. ___
up ___ and I screamed a - loud, ___
Bsus2
E
we'll take the world _ to - geth - er, we'll
We'll take a walk _ to - geth - er,
"Don't wanna be part of ___ your prob - lem, don't wanna
Bsus2
E/B
F#
take 'em by ___ the hand. ___
walk the road _ a - while." ___
be part of ___ your crowd." ___
'Cause I got a
E
B
hand for you. ___
1.
2., 3. I got a hand for you. ___

F♯
E
B
1
I wan-na run with you.
Yes - ter -
2,3
(Won't you let me run with you.)
Hold
E
F♯
my hand.
(Want you to hold my hand.)
B
E
F♯
Hold my hand.
I'll take you
I'll take you

B
E
F♯
Hold
my
hand.
(to a place where you can be)
(to the prom - ised land.)
E
an - y - thing you wan - na be be - cause
May - be we can't change the world, but
I wan - na
Bsus2
To Coda
E
love you the best that, the best that I can.
Bsus2
E
Bsus2
E

B
E/B
D.S. al Coda
See, I was
CODA
Bsus2
E/B
Bsus2
E
Yeah.
Guitar solo
Bsus2
E
B
E
F♯
E
B
Solo ends

B
E
F♯
Hold my hand. Want you to
hold my hand. Hold my hand.
I'll take you
I'll take you
Hold my hand.
to a place where you can be
to the prom - ised land.
an - y - thing you wan - na be be - cause I,
May - be we can't change the world, but
1
E

2
E
oh,
no, no, no.
I wan - na
Bsus2
E
love you the best that, the best that I can,
Bsus2
E
oh,
the best that I can.
Bsus2
E
Bsus2
E/B

Hold On

Words and Music by Carnie Wilson, Chynna Phillips and Glen Ballard
Moderate Rock
F C/F B♭(add9)/F C/F F C/F B♭(add9)/F
mf
F C/F B♭/F F F/E Dm7 F(add9)/A B♭
I know there's pain. Why do you lock your-self up in these chains?
You could sus - tain. Mm, or are you com-f'rta - ble with the pain?
B♭/C F C/F B♭/F C/F
No one can change your life ex - cept for you. Don't
You've got no one to blame for your un - hap - pi-ness. No, ba - by,
F C/F B♭/F C
ev - er let an - y - one step all o - ver you. Just
you got your - self in - to your own mess, ooh,

F
C/F
B♭/F
C/E
o - pen your heart and your mind, mm.
let - tin' your wor - ries pass you by, ba - by.
Dm
F(add9)/A
B♭
B♭/C
Is it real-ly fair to feel this way in - side? Woh,
Don't you think it's worth your time to change your mind? No, no,
F
B♭/F
C/F
F
Some day some-bod-y's gon-na make you wan-na turn a-round and say good-bye.
B♭/F
C/F
F
Un-til then ba - by, are you gon-na let him hold you down and make you cry? Don't you know

B♭/F
C/F
F
To Coda
don't you know things could change? Things-'ll go your way if you hold
B♭
F/A
Gm7
Gm7/C
B♭
F/A
on for one more day. Can you hold on for one
Gm7
Gm7/C
1
no chord
more day? Things-'ll go your way. Hold on for one more day.
F
C/F
B♭(add9)/F
C/F
F
C/F
B♭(add9)/F

2
no chord
F
C/F
B♭/F
Hold on for one more day.
I know that there is pain, but ya
C/F
F
C/F
B♭/F
hold on for one more day, and ya
break free from the chains.
F
C/F
B♭/F
C/F
Yeah, I know that there is pain, but ya
hold on for one more day, and ya
D.S. al Coda
CODA
B♭
F/A
break free break from the chains.
on for one

Gm7
Gm7/C
F
B♭/F
C/F
F
more day, yeah. Hold on.
B♭/F
C/F
F
B♭/F
Don't you know, things could change?
C/F
F
B♭
F/A
Things could go your way if you hold on for one
Gm7
Gm7/C
F
B♭/F
C/F
F
Repeat ad lib. and Fade
more day, if you hold on. Can you hold on?

From the Paramount and DreamWorks Motion Picture SAVING PRIVATE RYAN

Hymn To The Fallen

Music by John Williams

C
D
Bm
G/B
G6/B
C6/G
Am6
Gsus9/D
G
F♯m7♭5
Gsus9/B
G/B
D7sus4/A
D7/A
Gmaj7
G
Cmaj7
D
C
D
C
D
F♯m7♭5
Gsus9/B
G/B
D7sus4/A
D7/A
Gmaj7
G
Cmaj7
D
C
D
G
Gsus4 sus2
G
Gsus4 sus2
Slightly faster
G
D/G
mf

C/G D/G C/G D/G C/G D/G Cmaj7 D G
G G/A Gmaj7/B G/C C D/G C/G D/A C/E Gmaj7/F♯ C/G Am C Cmaj7/B
cresc.
Gmaj7 C F♯m7♭5 G/B D7sus4/A G D/F♯ D C D F♯m7♭5 G/B D7sus4/A
f
Em/G D6/F♯ Em D C Am7/D D G
dim.
mf
G Gmaj7 D/G Em/G D/G C/G D/G
p

C D G Bm/F♯ D/F♯ Em D C D
D/G C D Bm G/B Em/B Am7 D7 Gadd2 G F♯m7♭5 Gsus9/B G/B
mp
D7sus4/A D7/A Gmaj7 G Cmaj7 D/G C D C D
F♯m7♭5 Gsus9/B G/B D7sus4/A D7/A Gmaj7 G Cmaj7 D/G C D
mf
G
cresc.

Broadly and expansively
G
Gmaj7
D/G
Em/G
D/G
C
D
f
C
D
Bm
Am7
D7
Gadd2
G
F♯m7♭5
Gsus9/B
G/B
D7sus4/A
Gmaj7
G
Cmaj7
D/C
C
D
C
D
F♯m7♭5
G/B
Am7
Gmaj7
C
G/B
Am7
Em/G
Em
D6/F♯
Em
D
C
Bm/D
C
D
dim.

G
Dadd4 D/G G
mf
mp
C/G D/G
C D Gmaj7
Cadd♭5 C/E
G D/G
Am7 Am7/C Dadd4
G
G sus4 sus2
G
G sus4 sus2
G5
p
G

I'd Do Anything For Love (But I Won't Do That)

Words and Music by Jim Steinman

D
Asus/E
Asus
an - y - thing for love. I'll nev - er lie to you and
D
A/D
G(add9)/D
Bm
that's a fact. But I'll nev - er for - get the way you
F♯m/A
G(add9)
A
feel right now, oh no, no way. And I would do
D
Asus/E
D/A
A
G(add9)
an - y - thing for love, but I won't do that.

Tempo I
Asus
D
No, I won't do that.
Gmaj7
A
Bm
Some days it don't come eas - y,
Some nights you're breath - ing fire,
Some days I pray for si - lence,
G(add9)
some days it don't come hard.
some nights you're carved in ice.
some days I pray for soul.

Em7
Some days it don't come at all and
Some nights are like noth - ing I've ev - er
Some days I just pray to the God of
D
1
2, 3
these are the days that nev - er end.
seen be - fore or will a - gain.
Sex and Drums and Rock 'n Roll.
G
D
Bm7
May - be I'm cra - zy, but it's cra - zy and it's
May - be I'm lone - ly, and that's all I'm qual - i - fied to
(Half-time feel)
Asus
A
G
D
true. I know you can save me. No one else can
be. There's just one and on - ly, the one and on - ly

Bm
Asus
A
Em
save me now __ but you.
promise I ____ can keep.
As long as the plan -
As long as the wheels _
(End half-time feel)
C#dim7
- ets are turn - ing,
____ are turn - ing,
as long as the stars ____ are burn - ing,
as long as the fires ____ are burn - ing,
G
A7
as long as your dreams _ are com - ing true,
as long as your prayers _ are com - ing true,
you bet - ter be - lieve _
you bet - ter be - lieve _
Tempo II
D
Gsus2
Asus
___ it that I would do an - y - thing _ for love.
___ it that I would do an - y - thing _ for love
Oh, I would do
and you know it's true and
molto rall.

D
Gsus2
Asus/E
Asus
To Coda
G(add9)
Tempo I
Bm
G
1
A
an - y - thing _ for love. Oh, I would do an - y - thing _ for love,
that's a fact. I would do an - y - thing _ for love,
but I won't do ___ that. No, I won't do ___
and there'll nev - er be no
that. I would _ do an - y - thing _ for love, an - y - thing you've _
___ been dream - ing of, but I ___ just won't ___ do ______

2
A
D.S. al Coda
won't do...
CODA
D
A
G
turn-ing back.
But I'll
Bm
F♯m/A
G(add9)
nev - er do it bet - ter than I do it with you. _ So long, so
A
D
Gsus2
A
long. And I would do an - y - thing _ for love. Oh, I would do
D
Gsus2
Asus/E
an - y - thing _ for love. ______ I would do
D
Gsus2
A
an - y - thing _ for love,

G(add9)
Asus
but I won't do ___ that, no, no, no, I won't do ___
(Girl:) Will you
D
Gsus2
Asus
D
Gsus2
Asus/E
that.
raise me up, ___ will you help ___ me down? Will you get me right out ___ of the God-
ca-ter to ev - 'ry fan-ta - sy I got? Will you hose me down with ho - ly wat - er
D
Gsus2
Asus
A
- for-sak - en town? Will you make it all a lit - tle less ___ cold? (Boy:) I can do ___
if I get too hot? Will you take me plac - es I've nev - er gone? (Boy:) I can do ___
G(add9)
1
Asus
2
Asus
that, oh ______ no ___ I can do
that, oh _____ (Girl:) Will you ___ no ___ I can do

D
Gsus2
Asus
D
Gsus2
that.
I know the ter - ri tor - y. I've been a-round. It-'ll all turn to dust and we'll all
Asus/E
D
Gsus2
A
D/A
Asus
fall down. Soon-er or lat - er you'll be screw-ing a-round. (Boy:) I won't do
Slower
Gsus2
Asus
D
Gsus2/D
Asus/E
that. No, I won't do that.
An - y - thing for love,
D/A
A7
D
but I won't do that.

I'll Make Love To You

Words and Music by Babyface

A/G
F♯m7
D/F♯
A/G
out the can - dle - light ___ for to - night is just your
got no - where to go. ___ I'm just gonna con - cen - trate on
F♯m7
Dm/F
Em7
Gmaj7/A
night. _ We're gon - na cel - e - brate all through the night. Pour the
you. ___ Girl, are you read - y? It's gonna be a long night. Throw your
D
Bm7
2fr
A/G
wine, __ light the fire. ____ Girl, your wish is my com -
clothes _ on the floor ____ I'm gonna take my clothes off
F♯m7
D/F♯
A/G
F♯m7
Dm/F
mand. _ I sub - mit to your de - mands. _____ I will do
too. ___ I made plans to be with you. _____ Girl, what -

Em7
Gmaj7/A
D
an - y - thing. Girl, you need on - ly ask.
ev - er you ask me, you know I could do.
I'll make love to you like you
Bm7
2fr
Em7
G/A
A
want me to and I'll hold you tight, ba - by, all through the night. I'll make
D
Bm7
2fr
Em
D
To Coda
love to you when you want me to and I will not let go till you
1
C
Gmaj7/A
tell me to.
Girl, re

2
C
F♯m7
B/D♯
4 fr
tell me to. Ba - by, to - night is your night and I
Em7
A9sus
A/G
F♯m7
will do you right. Just make a wish on your
B/D♯
4 fr
Em7
D
night, an - y - thing that you ask. I will
C
Gmaj7/A
D.S. al Coda
give you the love of your life, your life, your life. I'll make

CODA
C
Asus
D
tell me to. I'll make love to you like you
Instrumental ad lib. and Fade
Bm7
2fr
Em7
G/A
A
want me to. and I'll hold you tight, ba - by, all through the night. I'll make
D
Bm7
2fr
Em
D
love to you when you want me to and I will not let go till you
C
Gmaj7/A
Repeat ad lib. and Fade
tell me to.

I'll Stand By You

Words and Music by Chrissie Hynde, Tom Kelly and Billy Steinberg

F♯m
Bm
F♯m
Bm
When the night_falls on you, you don't know_what to do, noth-ing you con-
G
A
D
fess could make me love you less. I'll stand by you, I'll stand by
Bm7
2fr
Am7
G
D
F
G
you, won't let no-bod-y hurt_you,_ I'll stand by you.
C
Em
So, if you're mad,_ get mad;_ don't hold it all in-

F
C/G
G/B
C
Am
side, come on and talk to me now. And hey, what you got to
Em
F
Am
G
3
hide? I get an-gry too, well, I'm a lot like you. When you're
Em
Am
Em
Am
stand - ing at the cross - roads and don't know which path to choose, let me come a -
F
G7sus
long, 'cause e - ven if you're wrong, I'll stand by

D
Bm7
2fr
Am7
G
you, I'll stand by you, won't let no-bod-y hurt _ you. _ I'll stand by
D
Bm7
2fr
Am7
G
you, take me in in-to your dark-est hour, _ and I'll nev-er de-sert _ you, _ I'll stand by
D
Bm7
2fr
G
you.
Bm
A
F♯m
Bm
And when, when the night falls _

F♯m
Bm
G
A
A/C♯
on you, ba - by, you're feel-ing all a - lone, you won't be on your own. I'll stand by
D
Bm7
2fr
you, I'll stand by you, won't let no-bod - y hurt
Am7
G
D
you. I'll stand by you, take me in in - to your
Repeat and Fade
Bm7
2fr
Am7
G
dark - est hour, and I'll nev-er de - sert you. I'll stand by

Tears In Heaven

D/F#
A/E
E
if I saw you in heav - en?
if I saw you in heav - en?
if I saw you in heav - en?
F#m
C#/E#
Em6
(1.,3.) I must be strong
and car - ry on
(2.) I'll find my way
through night and day
F#
Bm
'cause I know
I don't be - long
'cause I know
I just can't stay
E7sus
To Coda
A
E/G#
F#m
A/E
here in heav - en.
here in heav - en.
3

1
D/F♯
E7sus
E7
A
2
D/F♯
E7sus
E7
A
C
Bm
Time can bring you down,
Am
D/F♯
G
D/F♯
Em
D/F♯
G
time can bend your knees.
C
Bm
Am
D/F♯
G
D/F♯
Time can break the heart,
have you beg - gin' please,
beg-gin' please.

E
A
E/G♯
F♯m
F♯m/E
D/F♯
A/E
E
A
E/G♯
F♯m
F♯m/E
D/F♯
A/E
E
F♯m
C♯/E♯
Em6
Be - yond the door
there's peace, I'm sure,

F♯
Bm
E7sus
and I know there'll be no more tears in heav-
A
E/G♯
F♯m
A/E
D/F♯
E7sus
E7
en.
A
D.S. al Coda
CODA
A
E/G♯
F♯m
en.
A/E
D/F♯
E7sus
E7
A
rall.

If I Ever Lose My Faith In You

Written and Composed by Sting

Asus2
A
G
You could say I lost my be - lief in the ho - ly___ church.
You could say I lost my ___ faith in the peo - ple on T. V.
that did - n't go from a bless-ing to a curse.
Dsus2(sus4)
D
Dsus2(sus4)
D
Asus2
A
You could say I
You could say I lost my be -
I nev - er saw no
G
Dsus2(sus4)
D
Dsus2(sus4)
D
To Coda
lost __ my sense of di-rect - ion.
lief __ in our pol-i-ti - cians.
mil-i-tar-y sol-u-tion
Asus2
A
F#m7
You could say all of this and worse, but
They all seem like game show hosts to me.

Esus2
E
F#7sus
F#7
G6
if
If
I ev - er lose my faith in you
Asus
A
A/B
Esus2
E
F#7sus
F#7
there'd be noth - ing left for me to do.
G6
1 Asus
A
2 Asus
A
Asus
A
Hey, hey.
G5
E5
G5
E5
G5
E5
172

G5
E5
F#m7
G#m7(add4)
I could be lost in - side their
Amaj9
Bsus
B
F#sus2
F#
lies with - out a trace, but ev - 'ry
G#7sus
G#7
B/A
A
B/A
A6
D.S. al Coda
time I close my eyes I see your face.
CODA
Asus2
A
F#m7
that did-n't al-ways end up as some-thing worse, but

Esus2 E C#m7
let me say this first:
Bsus2 B C#7sus C#7 D6
if I ev-er lose my faith in you, if I ev-er lose
Esus E Bsus2 B C#7sus C#7
my faith in you there'd be noth-ing left for me to do,
D6 Esus E Esus2 E
there'd be noth-ing left for me to do. If I ev-er lose

F#7sus
F#7
G6
Asus
A
A/B
my faith,
if I ev - er lose my faith,
Esus2
E
F#7sus
F#7
G6
if I ev - er lose my faith,
if I ev - er lose
Asus
A
Asus
A
G5
E5
my faith
in you...
G5
E5
G5
E5
G5
E5
Repeat and Fade

Ironic

Lyrics by Alanis Morissette

Music by Alanis Morissette and Glen Ballard

Moderate Rock

Fmaj7 G6 Fmaj7

mp

G/B C(add2) G/B Am7

An old man_ turned nine-ty - eight._ He won the
Play It Safe was a-fraid to fly. He packed his
traf - fic jam when you're al - read-y late._ A no -

mp - mf

G/B C(add2) G/B Am7

lot - ter - y, and died the next_ day. It's a
suit - case and kissed his kids good - bye. He wait-ed
smok-ing sign on your cig - ar - ette break. It's like

G/B C(add2) G/B Am7

black fly____ in your Char - don - nay._ It's a
his whole damn life to take that flight, and as the
ten thou - sand spoons when all you need is a knife. It's

G/B
C(add2)
To Coda
G/B
Am7
death row pardon two minutes too late.
plane crashed down, he thought, "Well, isn't this nice..."
meeting the man of my dreams, and then
Isn't it ironic... don't you think?
It's like rain on your wedding day.
G
C
It's a free ride when you're already paid.
It's the good advice
f

G
C
G
Am7
that you just did - n't take.
Bb
F
1
G
Who would - 've thought... it fig - ures.
Mis - ter
mf
2
G
Fmaj7
Well, life has a fun - ny way of sneak - ing up on
mf
G6
Fmaj7
you when you think ev - 'ry - thing's O. K. and ev - 'ry - thing's go - ing right.

G6
Fmaj7
And life has a fun - ny way of help-ing you out
when you think ev-'ry-thing's gone wrong and ev-'ry-thing blows up in your face.
C
D.S. al Coda
A
CODA
G/B
Am7
meet-ing his beau - ti - ful wife.
G/B
C(add2)
And is - n't it i - ron - ic... don't you
mp

G/B Am7 G/B C(add2)
think? A lit-tle too i-ron-ic... and yeah, I
G/B Am7 G C
real-ly do think... it's like rain on your
f
G Am7 G C
wed-ding day. It's a free ride when you're
G Am7 G C
al-read-y paid. It's the good ad-vice that you

G
Am7
B♭
F
G
just did - n't take.
And who would have thought, it fig-ures.
dim.
Fmaj7
G6
Fmaj7
And you know life has a fun-ny way of sneak-ing up on
mp
G6
Fmaj7
G6
you.
Life has a fun - ny, fun - ny way
of help - ing you out,
Fmaj7
help - ing you out.

Let Her Cry

Words and Music by Darius Carlos Rucker, Everett Dean Felber,
Mark William Bryan and James George Sonefeld

G
D
She nev-er lets me in,
on-ly tells me where she's been
This morn-ing I woke up a-lone,
found a note stand-ing by the phone
Last night I tried to leave,
cried so much, I could not be-lieve
C(add9)
G
when she's had too much to drink.
say-in', "May-be, may-be I'll be back some day."
she was the same girl I fell in love with long a-go.
D
I say that I don't care, I just run my hands through her dark hair, and I
I want-ed to look for you, you walked in. I did-n't know just what to do, so I
She went in the back to get high. I sat down on my couch and cried, yell-ing,

C(add9)
G
pray to God you got-ta help me fly a - way.
sat back down, had a beer and felt sor - ry for my - self.
"Oh, ma - ma, please help me. Won't you hold my hand?"
And just
Say - in',
And
let her cry
C(add9)
G
if the tears fall down like rain.
Let her sing
C(add9)
Em
G
D
if it eas - es all her pain.
Let her go,
C(add9)
G
let her walk right out on me.
And if the

D
1,2
C
To Coda
sun comes up to-mor - row, let her be,
let her be.
oh.
G
D
C
G
3 G
D.S. al Coda
Let her cry
CODA
C
G
oh, let her be.

Linger

Lyrics by Dolores O'Riordan
Music by Dolores O'Riordan and Noel Hogan

C
rude, but it's just your at - ti - tude. It's tear-ing me a - part,
G
it's ru - in - ing ev - 'ry - thing. I swore,
D
I swore I would be true and hon - ey, so did you.
if you could get by try - ing not to lie,
A
So, why were you hold - ing her
things would - n't be so con -

C
hand?_ Is that the way_ we stand?__ Were you ly - ing all__ the time?__
fused __ and I would - n't feel_ so used,__ but you al - ways real - ly knew__
G
Was it just a game_ to you?__
I just wan - na be__ with you.__
But I'm in ______ so
D
deep.
You know I'm such a fool __ for you.
A
You got me wrapped a - round your fin - ger,__ ah,____ ha,___ ha.
C

G
Do you have to let it lin - ger? Do you have to, do you
D
To Coda
have to, do you have to let it lin - ger?
A6
Oh, I thought the world of you. I thought
Instrumental solo
C
noth - ing could go wrong, but I was wrong.

G
1
I was wrong.
If you,
2
D.S. al Coda
(End Solo) And I'm in so
CODA
D
ger?
ger? Instrumental solo
A
You know I'm such a fool for you.
C
You got me wrapped a - round your fin - ger, ah, ha, ha.

G
Do you have to let it lin - ger? Do you have to, do you
1
2
D
have to, do you have to let it lin-
Gmaj7/D
D
Gmaj7/D
D
Gmaj7/D
D

From the Paramount and Twentieth Century Fox Motion Picture TITANIC

My Heart Will Go On (Love Theme From 'Titanic')

Music by James Horner

Lyric by Will Jennings

E
B
Asus2
Far a-cross the dis-tance and spac-es be-
E/B
B
E
B
A
tween us you have come to show you go on.
C♯m
B(add4)
A
Near, far, wher-ev-er you are,
B
C♯m
B(add9)
A
I be-lieve that the heart does go on.
4fr
7fr

B
C♯m
4fr
B
A
Once more you o - pen the door
B
C♯m
4fr
G♯m
4fr
A
and you're here in my heart, and my heart will go
To Coda
Bsus
2fr
B
C♯m7
4fr
Bsus
2fr
A
on and on.
Bsus
2fr
B
E
B
Asus2
Love can touch us one time and last for a

E/B
B
E
B
A
life - time, and nev-er let go till we're gone.
E
B
Asus2
Love was when I loved you; one true time I
E/B
G#7/B#
C#m
G#m
A
hold to. In my life we'll al - ways go on.
D.S. al Coda
CODA
C#m7
Bsus
on.

A
Bsus
B
C♯m7
Bsus
A
C♯m/G♯
G♯7/F♯
Fm
E♭
You're here, there's
D♭
E♭
Fm
E♭
noth - ing I fear and I know that my heart will go
D♭
E♭sus
E♭
Fm
E♭
on. We'll stay for -
f

Db
Eb
Fm
Cm7
ev - er this way. You are safe in my heart, and my
Db
Ab/Eb
Eb
Ab
Eb/Ab
heart will go on and on.
ff decrescendo to end
Db/Ab
Eb/Ab
Ab
Eb/Ab
Mm.
Db/Ab
Ab(add9)

The Power Of Love

Words by Mary Susan Applegate and Jennifer Rush
Music by Candy Derouge and Gunther Mende

E♭
3fr
as I look ___ in your eyes.
A♭
4fr
I hold on ___ to your ___ bod-y ___
__ times ___
Fm
and feel each move you make.
it seems I'm far a - way,
D♭
Your voice is warm and ten - der, ___ a love that
nev - er won - der where I am 'cause I am

A♭/C
E♭
3 fr
I could not for - sake.
al - ways by your side.
A♭
4 fr
'Cause I'm your la - dy
and you are my man.
D♭
B♭m
When-ev - er you reach for me,
E♭
3 fr
I'll do
(D.S.) I'm gon-na do
all that I can.

1
2, 3
E-ven though there may be
We're head-ing for
Ab
4fr
some-thing,
some-where I've nev-er been.
Db
To Coda
Some-times I am fright-
Bbm
Eb
3fr
Db
Ab
4fr
-ened but I'm read-y to learn
'bout the pow-er of love.

D♭
E♭
3 fr
The sound of your heart
A♭
4 fr
beat - ing
made it clear sud-den -
Fm
ly.
The feel-ing that I can't go on
D.S. al Coda
is light years a - way.
'Cause I'm your la -

CODA
B♭m
E♭
3fr
D♭
- ened but I'm read - y to learn
'bout the pow - er of love.
A♭
4fr
The pow-er of love.
Repeat and Fade

Save The Best For Last

Words and Music by Phil Galdston, Jon Lind and Wendy Waldman

Cm
B♭
A♭
I see the pas - sion in your eyes.
You won - dered how you'd make it through.
Just when I thought a chance had passed,
E♭/G
A♭
B♭
To Coda
Some - times it's all a big sur - prise.
I won - dered what was wrong with you.
you go and save the best for last.
E♭
A♭
'Cause there was a time when all I did
'Cause how could you give your love to some -
E♭/G
Fm7
B♭7
was wish you'd tell me this was love.
one else and share your dreams with me?

E♭
3 fr
B♭m7
It's not the way I hoped or how
Some - times the ver - y thing you're look -
A♭/C
3 fr
D♭(add9)
4 fr
A♭/C
3 fr
I planned, but some - how it's e - nough.
- ing for is the one thing you can't see.
B♭
N.C.
B♭
A♭
4 fr
And now we're stand - ing face to face.
But now we're stand - ing face to face.
E♭/G
3 fr
A♭
4 fr
B♭
Is - n't this world a cra - zy place?

Cm
3 fr
Bb
Ab
4 fr
Just when I thought our chance had passed,
Eb/G
3 fr
Ab
4 fr
Bb
you go and save the best for last.
1
Ab(add9)
3 fr
Bbsus
Db6/9
Cm7
3 fr
Eb
3 fr
All of the nights
2
Eb
3 fr

A♭
E♭/G
A♭
B♭
La da da da da
Cm
A♭
E♭/G
da da.
A♭
B♭
E♭
Some - times the ver -
B♭m7
Cm7
- y thing you're look - ing for is the

Db(add9)
Ab/C
Bb
N.C.
D.S. al Coda
one thing you can't see.
Some - times the snow
CODA
Eb
Bb/D
Ab/C
Eb/Bb
Ab
Bb5
Ab(add9)
You went and saved the best for last.
Bbsus
Db6/9
Cm7
Eb
Yeah.

Say You'll Be There

Words and Music by Elliot Kennedy and Spice Girls

Am7
D9
4fr
(1.) Last time that we had this con - ver - sa - tion,
(2.) And now you tell me that you're fall - ing in love. Well, I
(D.S.) If you put two and two to - geth - er, you will

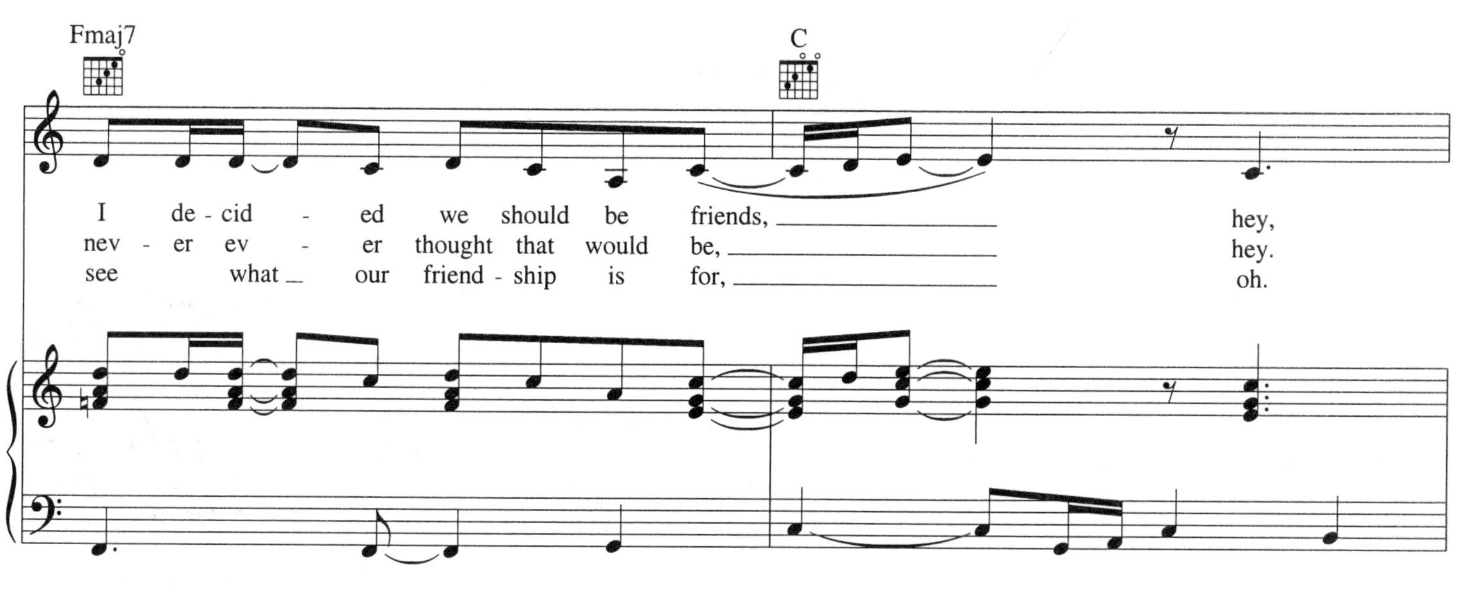
Fmaj7
C
I de - cid - ed we should be friends, hey,
nev - er ev - er thought that would be, hey.
see what our friend - ship is for, oh.

Am7
D9
4fr
but now, we're go - ing 'round in cir - cles. Tell me,
This time you got - ta take it eas - y, throw - ing
If you can work this e - qua - tion, then I'll

Fmaj7
1
C
will this déjà vu never end,
far too much emotions at me.
guess I'll have to show you the door.
oh?
2, 3
C
Bb/C
But any fool can see they're falling.
There is no need to say you love me.
Fmaj7
Ab/Bb
G9sus
3fr
I gotta make you understand.
It would be better left unsaid.
Am7
D9
4fr
I'm giving you ev'rything, all that joy

Fm6
C
can bring. This I swear.
(1.) I'll give you ev - 'ry - thing.
(2.) Yes, I swear.
Am7
D9
4 fr
And all that I want from you is a prom -
To Coda
Fm6
C
- ise you will be there. Say you will be there,
Am
D
Am
yeah. Ow. Say you will be there.

D
D.S. al Coda
(take 2nd ending)
Won't you sing it with me?
CODA
C
Yeah, I
Am7
D9
4 fr
Fmaj7
1
C
want you.
Instrumental solo
Vocal 1st time only
2
C
B♭/C
Fmaj7
Solo ends
An - y fool can see they're fall - ing. I got - ta
A♭/B♭
G9sus
3 fr
make you un - der - stand. I'll

N.C.
give you ev - 'ry-thing, on this I swear, just prom - ise you'll al - ways be there.
Am7
D9
4 fr
I'm giv - ing you ev - 'ry - thing, all that joy
Lead vocal ad lib.
Fm6
C
Am7
can bring. This I swear. And all that I want
D9
4 fr
Fm6
C
Repeat and Fade
from you is a prom - ise you will be there.

From JEKYLL & HYDE

Someone Like You

Words by Leslie Bricusse
Music by Frank Wildhorn

F C/F B♭/F F C/F A/C♯
the past is hold-ing me, keep-ing life at bay. I wan-der, lost in yes - ter-
to help me see a world I've nev-er seen be-fore, a love to o-pen ev - 'ry
Dm Dm/C B♭ Gm7 B♭/C
day, want - ing to fly, but scared to try. But if
door, to set me free, to let me soar. For if
F Gm7
some - one like you found some - one like me, then
mf
Fsus4 F/A B♭ Gm7♭5
sud - den - ly nothing would ev - er be the same. My
There'd be a

F
Gm7
F/A
Gm7
heart would take wing,
and I'd feel so a - live,
if
new way to live
and a new life to love,
if
1.
F
Dm
Gm7
D♭/E♭
Fadd2
Em7
G/A
A
some-one like you
found
me.
2.
F
Dm
Gm7
C7sus4
D♭maj7
C♭/D♭
some - one like you
found
me.
Oh, if
cresc.
G♭
A♭m7
some - one like you found some - one like me, then
f

G♭sus4
G♭/B♭
G♭
C♭maj7
A♭m7♭5
sud - den - ly nothing would ev - er be the same. My
G♭
E♭m
A♭m7
B♭m7
D♭/E♭
E♭7
heart would take wing, and I'd feel so a - live, if
rit.
Slower, freely
A♭m7
D♭sus4
G♭add2
C♭maj7
some-one like you loved me, loved
mp
G♭add2
C♭maj7
N.C.
G♭add2
me, loved me.

Something To Talk About (Let's Give Them Something To Talk About)

Words and Music by Shirley Eikhard

* Recorded a half step lower

A
I just ig - nore it, but they keep say - ing we
Now I'm con - vinced I'm go - ing un - der.
F♯m
G
F♯m
laugh just a lit - tle too loud, we stand just a lit - tle too close,
Think-ing 'bout you ev - er - y day, dream - ing 'bout you ev - 'ry night.
G
C
F
we stare just a lit - tle too long.
I'm hop - ing that you feel the same way.
E
May - be they're see - ing some - thing we don't, dar - ling.
Now that we know it, let's real - ly show it, dar - ling.

A
E
Let's give them some - thing to talk a - bout.
Let's give them some - thing to talk a - bout,
A
E
Let's give them some - thing to talk a - bout.
a lit - tle mys - t'ry to fig - ure out.
A
E
F♯m
Let's give them some - thing to talk a - bout. How a - bout love?
Let's give them some - thing to talk a - bout. How a - bout love,
G
D
1.
F
2.
F
love, love?

C
G
Let's give them some - thing to talk a - bout,
C
G
a lit - tle mys - t'ry to fig - ure out.
C
G
Am
Let's give them some - thing to talk a - bout.
How a - bout love?
B♭
F
A♭
4fr.
Repeat and fade

From the Paramount Motion Picture ANDRE

Thanks To You

Words and Music by Julie Gold

* Recorded a half step lower

C G/B Am7 C/D
there is noth - ing that I could not do, thanks to you,
G G/B Am7 C/D
for teach - ing me how to feel, show - ing me my e - mo -
mp
G G/B Am7 C/D
tions, let - ting me know what's real from what is not.
C G/B Am7 C/D
What I've got is more than I'd ev - er hoped for,

C G/B Am7 C/D
and a lot of what I've hoped for is thanks to you.
G C G/B Am7 C/D G
No moun - tain, no val - ley, no time, no space, no heart -
mf
C G/B Am7 C/D C G/B
ache, no heart - break, no fall from grace can stop me from be - liev - ing that my
Am7 C/D D/E
love will pull me through, thanks to you. Thanks to you
3

A
A/C♯
Bm7
D/E
for teach - ing me how to live,
put - ting things in per- spec-
tive,
show - ing me how to give
and how to take.
D
No mis - take
we were
put here to - geth - er.
E
And if I break- down,
for - give me, but it's true
f

D
A/C♯
Bm7
that I am ach - ing with the love I feel in -
D/E
side,
thanks to you,
mp
A
Bm7
A/C♯
D
A/C♯
Bm7
you,
rit.
Freely, slowly
D/E
E
A
thanks to
you.

From JEKYLL & HYDE

This Is The Moment

Words by Leslie Bricusse
Music by Frank Wildhorn

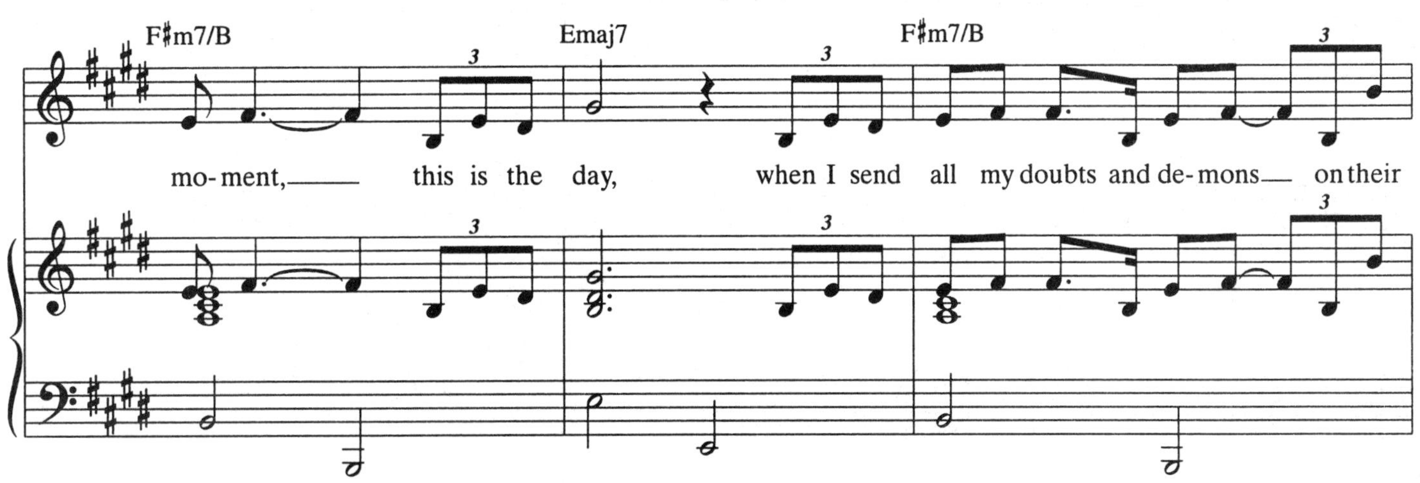

F♯m7
E/G♯
A
B7sus4
com - ing in - to play, is here and now to - day. This is the
F♯m7/B
Emaj7
F♯m7/B
mo - ment, this is the time when the mo - men - tum and the mo - ment are in
mp
Emaj7
C♯madd2
G♯m
rhyme. Give me this mo - ment, this pre - cious chance. I'll
F♯m7
E/G♯
A
A/B
B7
gath - er up my past and make some sense at last. This is the

E
F♯m7/E
F♯m7♭5/E
mo - ment when all I've done, all of the
mo - ment, my fi - nal test. Des - ti - ny
mf
C♯m
Amaj7
B/A
dream - ing, schem - ing and scream - ing be - come one! This is the
beck - oned, I nev - er reck - oned sec - ond best. I won't look
F♯m7
G♯m7
To Coda
day, see it spar - kle and shine, when all I've
down, I must not fall. This is the
F♯m7/B
Esus4
A
E/G♯
lived for be - comes mine! For all these years I've

B/A E/G♯ F♯m7 E/G♯
faced the world a - lone, and now the time has come to
Am Bsus4 A/B
D.S. al Coda
prove to them I made it on my own. This is the
Coda
F♯m7 E/G♯ F♯m7 F♯m7/B B7 E C7
mo-ment, the sweet-est mo-ment of them all! This is the
F Gm7/F F Gm7♭5/F
mo - ment. Damn all the odds. This day or

F
Dm7
B♭maj7
C/B♭
nev - er, I'll sit for - ev - er with the gods!
When I look
Gm7
C/B♭
Am7
C/D
Dm
back,
I will al - ways re - call
mo - ment for
Gm7
F/A
B♭
F/A
Gm7
B♭/C
C7
mo - ment,
this was the mo - ment
the great - est mo - ment of them
Gm7/F
G7/F
Gm7/F
Gm7/C
F
all.
ff
rit.

To Be With You

Words and Music by Eric Martin and David Grahame

D
B
come on, ba - by, come on o - ver. Let me be the one to show you.
come on, ba - by, come on o - ver. Let me be the one to hold you.
E
A
B
E
A
I'm the one who wants to be with you.
Deep in - side I hope you'll
B
E
A
B
E
feel it, too.
Wait-ed on a line of greens and blues
A
1 B
E
2 B
E
just to be the next to be with you.
be with you.

A(add9)
C#m
Why be a - lone _ when we can be to-geth - er, ba - by?
G
You can make _ my life _ worth - while. _ I can make _ you start to
E
A
B
E
smile.
A
B
E

A
B
C♯m
E
A
B
E
When
A(add9)
E
A
E
it's through, it's through. And fate will twist the both of you. So
D
B
come on, ba - by, come on o - ver. Let me be the one to show you.
rit.

G
C
D
G
C
I'm the one who wants to be with you.
Deep in - side I hope you'll
a tempo
D
G
C
feel it, too.
Wait - ed on a line of
D
Em
G
C
greens and blues
just to be the next to
D
G
E
A
be with you.
I'm the one who wants to

B
E
A
be with you.
Deep in - side I hope you'll
feel it, too.
Wait - ed on a line of
C#m
greens and blues
just to be the next to
be with you,
just to be the next to
be with you.
Ooh.
rall.

Waterfalls

Words and Music by Marqueze Etheridge, Lisa Nicole Lopes,
Rico R. Wade, Pat Brown and Ramon Murray

D♭maj7
A♭(add9)
3fr
B♭
at a son that she just can't touch.
ta - tion, but he just can't ___ see.
If at an - y
E♭
3fr
B♭(add9)
6fr
time he's in a jam she'll be by his side,
She gives him lov - ing that his bod - y can't
but he does - n't
han - dle, but all
D♭maj7
A♭(add9)/E♭
6fr
re - al - ize he hurts her so much.
he can say is, "Ba - by, it's good to me."
E♭maj7
3fr
B♭(add9)
6fr
But all the pray - ing just ain't help - ing at all,
One day he goes and takes a glimpse in the mir - ror,
'cause he can't
but he

D♭maj7
A♭(add9)
3fr
seem to keep his self out of trou - ble. So, he goes out
does - n't rec - og - nize his own face.
E♭maj7
3fr
B♭(add9)
6fr
and he makes his mon - ey the best way he knows how, an - oth - er
His health is fad - ing and he does - n't know why. Three let - ters
D♭maj7
A♭(add9)
3fr
bod - y lay - ing cold in the gut - ter. Lis - ten to me.
took him to his fi - nal rest - ing place. Y'all don't hear me.
E♭
3fr
B♭(add9)
6fr
Don't go chas - ing wa - ter - falls. Please stick to the

D♭maj7
A♭(add9)
3fr
riv - ers and the lakes that you're used ___ to. I know that you're
E♭
3fr
B♭(add9)
6fr
gon - na have it your way or noth - ing at all, but I think you're
D♭maj7
A♭(add9)/E♭
6fr
1.
2.
mov-ing too fast. _
Come on. _
E♭maj7
3fr
B♭(add9)
6fr
D♭maj7
A♭
4fr
Rap (See additional lyrics)

E♭maj7
3fr
B♭(add9)
6fr
D♭maj7
A♭(add9)/E♭
6fr
1.
2.
no chord
Rap ends
E♭
3fr
B♭(add9)
6fr
Don't go chas - ing wa - ter - falls. Please stick to the
D♭maj7
A♭(add9)
3fr
riv - ers and the lakes that you're used to. I know that you're

Additional Lyrics

Rap: **I seen a rainbow yesterday**
But too many storms have come and gone
Leavin' a trace of not one God-given ray
Is it because my life is ten shades of gray
I pray all ten fade away
Seldom praise Him for the sunny days
And like His promise is true
Only my faith can undo
The many chances I blew
To bring my life to anew
Clear blue and unconditional skies
Have dried the tears from my eyes
No more lonely cries
My only bleedin' hope
Is for the folk who can't cope
Wit such an endurin' pain
That it keeps 'em in the pourin' rain
Who's to blame
For tootin' caine in your own vein
What a shame
You shoot and aim for someone else's brain
You claim the insane
And name this day in time
For fallin' prey to crime
I say the system got you victim to your own mind
Dreams are hopeless aspirations
In hopes of comin' true
Believe in yourself
The rest is up to me and you

When I Fall In Love

Words by Edward Heyman
Music by Victor Young

A7sus
A7♭9
6fr
Dm
Gm6
3fr
gun, and too man - y moon - light kiss - es seem to
Dm
G6/B
F/G
Steadily, with feeling
C
cool in the warmth of the sun. When I give my
Fm/C
C
Fm6/C
6fr
C7♭9
heart it will be com -
Am6/C
2fr
G7♭9
4fr
C
Dm7
Em7
Fmaj7
B♭/A
A+
- plete-ly, or I'll nev - er give my

C/D
D6
Fmaj7/G
G7♭9
4 fr
heart. Don't let me give my heart. And the
C
Am7
F#m7♭5
4fr
B7♭5
D/E
A
mo - ment I can feel that you feel that way
Dm7
B♭7
C/G
Gm7♭5
5fr
too, I feel that way too, is when I fall in
F/G
G7♭9
4fr
C
G/A
love, I'll fall in love with you.

Dm7
Fm
C/D
G7sus
C
When I fall in
Fm6/C
love
C
B♭7
A7
it will be for -
Dm7
G9sus
- ev - er,
C
Dm7
Em7
Fmaj7
or I'll nev - er
B♭/A
A+
fall
C/D
D6
in love,
oh, I'll nev-er, nev-er fall

Fmaj7/G
G7♭9
4 fr
C
Am7
in love.
In a rest - less world like
B♭9
C
Gm/B♭
A7sus
A7♭9
6fr
this is,
love is end - ed be - fore it's be - gun,
and too
Dm7
Dm(maj7)
man - y moon - light kiss - es
seem to
Dm
A9sus
A13
4 fr
cool in the warmth of the sun.

D
Gm/D
When I give my heart
D
C7
B7
Em7
A7sus
A7
it will be com - plete - ly,
D
Em7
F♯m7
Gmaj7
C/B
B7♭9
or I'll nev - er give, I'll nev - er give my heart,
D/E
E6
A9sus
A7♭9
6 fr
oh, I'll nev - er give my heart. And the

D
Bm
A/G
C#7♭9
mo - ment
I can feel that you
F#m7
B7♭9
Freely
Em7
C9
feel that way too
is
D/A
Gm6/A
D7♭9/A
E7/A
Gm6/A
F/C
B♭m6/C
F7♭9/C
G7/C
B♭m6/C
when I fall in love,
when I fall in love,
D/A
Gm6/A
D7♭9/A
Bm6/A
D
E/D
Gm6/D
D
when I fall in love with you.
rit.

From THE PRINCE OF EGYPT

When You Believe (From The Prince Of Egypt)

Words and Music Composed by Stephen Schwartz
with Additional Music by Babyface

G
D/F♯
Em7
A/C♯
We were mov-ing moun - tains long_ be - fore we knew we could.
D
A/C♯
Bm
F♯m/A
There can be mir - a - cles,_ when you be - lieve._ Though hope is frail, it's
Gmaj7
F♯m/A
Em/A
D
A/C♯
hard to kill. Who knows what mir - a - cles_ you can a - chieve?_
Bm
F♯m7
Gmaj7
Em7
A
When you be - lieve, some - how you will. You will when_ you_ be - lieve._

Bm
Bm
A
In this time of fear, when
mf
F♯m7
Bm
Gmaj9
prayer so of - ten proves in vain, hope seems like the sum - mer birds, too
Em7
F♯m7
B
A/C♯
swift - ly flown a - way.
Yet now I'm stand - ing here, my
A/D
Esus4
G
D/F♯
heart so full I can't ex - plain,
seek - ing faith and speak - ing words I

Em7
A/C#
E
never thought I'd say:
There can be mir - a - cles,
B/D#
C#m
G#m/B
Amaj7
G#m/B
F#m/B
when you be - lieve.
Though hope is frail,
it's
hard to kill.
(When you be - lieve.)
E
B/D#
Who knows what mir - a - cles
you
can a - chieve?
(You can a -
C#m
G#m7
Amaj7
G#m7
When you be - lieve,
some - how
you will.
chieve?)

F♯m7
E
B/D♯
E
C♯m7
4fr.
You will when you be-lieve.
Amaj9
Bsus4
2fr.
B/A
A/C♯
B/D♯
They don't al - ways hap - pen when you ask.
3
Esus4
E
B/D♯
C♯m7
4fr.
A/C♯
B/D♯
And it's eas - y to give in to your fear.
Esus4
E
F♯m7
E/G♯
Asus2
But when you're blind - ed by your pain, can't see

B
C♯m7
4fr.
— your way— clear through— the rain, a small— but still re-sil-ient voice— says
3
A/B
G♯m/B F♯m/B
F♯
C♯/E♯
help is ver-y near.
There can be mir-a-cles, when you be-lieve.
cresc.
rit.
f a tempo
D♯m
6fr.
A♯m/C♯
4fr.
Bmaj7
A♯m/C♯ G♯m/C♯
F♯
Though hope is frail, it's hard to kill.
Who knows what mir-a-cles
C♯/E♯
D♯m
6fr.
F♯/A♯
Bmaj7
you can a-chieve? When you be-lieve, some-how you will,

D♯m
6fr.
F♯/A♯
G♯m7
4fr.
C♯
4fr.
D♯m
6fr.
C♯6
4fr.
now you will. You will when you be - lieve.
Bmaj7
Tacet
You will when you, you will when you be -
mf
F♯
D♯m
6fr.
F♯
lieve, just be - lieve, just be -
mp
D♯m
6fr.
F♯
lieve. You will when you be - lieve.

Where Have All The Cowboys Gone?

Words and Music by Paula Cole

N.C.
N.C.
Oh, ___ you get me read - y in your
don't you stay the eve - ning, kick
fi - n'lly sold the Chev - y when we
fif - ty - six Chev - y. Why don't we go sit down in the shade? _ Take
back and watch the T V, and I'll fix a lit - tle some-thing to eat. ___ Oh,
had an - oth - er ba - by and you took that job in Ten - nes - see. You
shel - ter on my front porch, the dan - de - li - on sun's scorch - in'
I know your back hurts from work - in' on the trac - tor. How
made friends at the farm and you join 'em at the bar al - most

Gmaj7
like a glass of cold lem-on-ade?
do you take your cof - fee, my sweet?
ev - 'ry sin - gle day of the week.
I will do the laun - dry if you pay all the bills.
I will raise the chil - dren if you pay all the bills.
I will wash the dish - es while you go have a beer.
A
Bm
C♯m
4fr
F♯m
Where is my John Wayne?
Where is my prai - rie sun?
Where is my hap - py end - ing?

D(add2)
To Coda
E(add2)
Bm7
2fr
Where have all the cow - boys gone?
C♯m
4fr
D(add2)
1
E(add2)
Why
2
E(add2)
Gmaj7
I am wear - ing my new dress
to-night, but you don't, but you don't e - ven no - tice
Bm

C♯m
4fr
D(add2)
E(add2)
me.
Say our good -
Bm7
2fr
C♯m
4fr
D(add2)
- byes,
say our good - byes,
say our good - byes.
E(add2)
N.C.
D.S. al Coda
Spoken: We
CODA
E(add2)
F♯m
- boys gone?
Where is my

C♯m
4 fr
F♯m
C♯m
4 fr
Marl - bor - o Man? _
Where is his shin - y gun?
F♯m
C♯m
4 fr
D(add2)
Where is my lone - ly ran - ger?
Where have all the cow -
E(add2)
Bm7
2 fr
C♯m
4 fr
Repeat ad lib.
- boys gone?
D(add2)
E

From SUNSET BOULEVARD

With One Look

Music by Andrew Lloyd Webber

Lyrics by Don Black and Christopher Hampton, with contributions by Amy Powers

A/C♯
Em7
A
D
A/E
E7
A
When I speak 'tis with my soul I can play a-ny role. No
E7/A
A
E7/A
D
A/C♯
Bm7
E
words can tell the stor-ies my eyes tell, watch me when I frown, you can't write that down. You
C
G/C
C
G
A
F♯m7
A
Bm7
E
know I'm right, it's there in black and white, when I look your way you'll hear what I say. Yes,
A
F♯m
Bm7
E
E7/D
with one look I put words to shame, just one look sets the screen a-flame.

A/C♯ Em7 A D A/C♯ Bm7 E7
Si - lent mu-sic starts to play, one tear in my eye makes the whole world cry.
A F♯m Bm7 D/E E7/D
With one look they'll for - give the past, they'll re - joice I've re-turned at last
f
A/C♯ Em A D A/E E7 A
to my peo-ple in the dark, still out there in the dark.
D Bm Em7 G/A A
f

D/F♯
Am
D
G
D/F♯
Em7
A
Si - lent mu-sic starts to play.
With one look you'll know all you need to know.
p
mf
D
Bm
Em7
G/A
A7/G
D/F♯
Am7
With one look I'll ig - nite a blaze, I'll re - turn to my glo - ry days. They'll say Nor-ma's back at
D
G9
G6
G
C
last.
This time I am stay-ing, I'm stay-ing for good, I'll be back where I was born to
mf marcato
Em
molto rit.
G/A
D
be, with one look I'll be___ me.___
f
ff

Wonderwall

Words and Music by Noel Gallagher

F♯m
A
Esus4
F♯m
I don't be - lieve that an - y - bo - dy feels the way I do a - bout you now.
Dmaj7
Esus4
F♯m
F♯m
A
Esus4
Bm
1. Back - beat the word was on the street that the fi - re in your heart is out.
(Verse 2 see block lyric)
F♯m
A
Esus4
Bm
I'm sure you've heard it all be - fore but you nev - er real - ly had a doubt.

F♯m
A
Esus4
Bm
I don't be - lieve that an - y - bo - dy feels the way I do a - bout you now.
F♯m
A
Esus4
Bm
And all
D
E
F♯m
the roads we have to walk are wind - ing and all
D
E
F♯m
the lights that lead us there are blind - ing.

D
E
A
/G♯
F♯m
There are ma - ny things_ that I_ would like to say to you_ but I don't know how,_
Bm
be - cause
I said
D
F♯m
A
F♯m
may - be_ you're gon - na be the one that
D
F♯m
A
F♯m
D
F♯m
saves me,_ and af - ter all

1.
A
F♯m
D
F♯m
A
A6
rall.
a tempo
— you're my won-der - wall.
2.
A
F♯m
D
F♯m
A
F♯m
I said may-be you're gon - na be the one that
D
F♯m
D
F♯m
D
F♯m
saves me, and af - ter all
A
F♯m
D
F♯m
A
F♯m
— you're my won-der - wall. I said

Verse 2:
Today was gonna be the day
But they'll never throw it back to you
By now you should've somehow
Realised what you're not to do
I don't believe that anybody
Feels the way I do
About you now.

And all the roads that lead you there were winding
And all the lights that light the way are blinding
There are many things that I would like to say to you
But I don't know how.

You Oughta Know

Lyrics by Alanis Morissette
Music by Alanis Morissette and Glen Ballard

F♯m7
ver - sion of me, is she per - vert - ed like me? Would she go
get a - bout me, Mis - ter Du - plic - i - ty? I hate to
Play both times
B/F♯
F♯m7
down on you in a the - a - ter? Does she speak el - o-quent-ly, and would she
bug you in the mid-dle of din-ner. It was a slap in the face, how quick-ly
B/F♯
have your ba - by? I'm sure she'd make a real - ly ex - cel - lent
I was re-placed, and are you think - ing of me when you
F♯m7
moth - er. 'Cause the love that you gave that we made was-n't a - ble to
fuck her? 'Cause the love that you gave that we made was-n't a - ble to
joke that you laid in the bed that was me and I'm

B/F♯
make it e-nough for you to be o - pen wide, no.
make it e-nough for you to be o - pen wide, no.
not gon-na fade as soon as you close your eyes, and you know
F♯m7
And ev - 'ry time you speak her name does she
And ev - 'ry time you speak her name does she
it. And ev - 'ry time I scratch my nails down some -
B/F♯
know how you told me you'd hold me un - til you died, till you died? But
know how you told me you'd hold me un - til you died, till you died? But
- one els - e's back, I hope you feel it. Well, can you
F♯
you're still a - live. And
you're still a - live. And
feel it? Well,
I'm here to re - mind

E
A
B
you of the mess you left when you went a-way. It's not
F♯
E
A
fair to de-ny me of the cross I bear that you gave
B
To Coda
1
N.C.
2
N.C.
to me. You, you, you ought-a know. ought-a know.
F♯m/B
B9
1-3

4
D.S. al Coda
'Cause the
CODA
ought - a know. I'm here
F♯
E
A
to re - mind you of the mess you left when you went
B
F♯
E
a - way. It's not fair to de - ny me of the cross
A
B
N.C.
I bear that you gave to me. You, you, you ought - a know.